Table of Cont

About the Author

Bud Smith is one of the most experienced and prolific authors writing about technology today. He has been on the cutting edge of technology introductions from the Intel 80386 microprocessor in the mid-1980s, to cutting-edge coverage of Web authoring in the 1990s, and the iPad 2 and the latest version of Facebook today. Bud has also written about climate change and planning and installing green roofs.

Bud's most recent title before this one is *Sams Teach Yourself Facebook for Business in 10 Minutes*, with in-depth coverage of the new fan page and other features that give businesses a voice on Facebook.

Bud began writing computer books back in 1984, the year of the iconic *1984* television commercial for the Macintosh. An early success was the *Computer Buyer's Guide* for Que, covering the then-latest and greatest in computer hardware and software. His books have sold more than a million copies in total.

Bud continues to work as a writer, project manager, and marketer to help people get the most out of technology as it advances. He currently lives in the San Francisco Bay Area, participating in environmental causes when he's not working on one of his many technology-related projects.

Dedication

This book is dedicated to Veronica, for successfully picking herself up by her bootstraps.

Acknowledgments

The first person to thank is Laura Norman, who helped tee up this book for fast, accurate delivery; to development editor Lora Baughey, for helping bring what may be the first mainstream book about the iPad 2 into being; to copy editor Barbara Hacha, for helping straighten snarled syntax; to technical editor Greg Kettell, for making sure everything said here is true and correct; and finally to the production team at Pearson, who applied their talents to bring my insights about using the iPad and iPad 2 into the useful and attractive *Teach Yourself* format. Also, my appreciation for the many people who are making this very cool new tool their own.

We Want to Hear from You!

As the reader of this book, *you* are our most important critic and commentator. We value your opinion and want to know what we're doing right, what we could do better, what areas you'd like to see us publish in, and any other words of wisdom you're willing to pass our way.

You can email or write me directly to let me know what you did or didn't like about this book—as well as what we can do to make our books stronger.

Please note that I cannot help you with technical problems related to the topic of this book, and that due to the high volume of mail I receive, I might not be able to reply to every message.

When you write, please be sure to include this book's title and author as well as your name and phone or email address. I will carefully review your comments and share them with the author and editors who worked on the book.

E-mail: consumer@samspublishing.com

Mail: Greg Wiegand
          Editor in Chief
          Sams Publishing
          800 East 96th Street
          Indianapolis, IN 46240 USA

Reader Services

Visit our website and register this book at informit.com/register for convenient access to any updates, downloads, or errata that might be available for this book.

Introduction

The iPad 2 and the original iPad, taken together, are the biggest thing to hit computing in years. Drawing on the best of Apple's iPhone and iPod touch products, and Apple's Macintosh personal computers, while introducing a whole new way of seeing and interacting with information, the two new devices have grabbed the imagination of the world.

The iPad 2 has taken the excitement about the original iPad to the next level. The iPad 2 is similar enough that the new iPad 2 and the original iPad are still one product line; they run the same operating software—which is also the same software as the latest iPhone and iPod Touch—and nearly all the same apps. Almost everything that you can do with an iPad 2, you can do with an iPad. The main exceptions, specific to the iPad 2, are taking photos, videoconferencing with FaceTime, and using games and a few other apps that take advantage of the iPad 2's three-axis gyroscope.

Using an iPad 2 is even more fun and satisfying than using the original iPad, thanks to a better overall design that is thinner, lighter, and easier to handle, as well as the new front-facing camera, rear-facing camera, and three-axis gyroscope.

One leading tech columnist said that the appeal of the original iPad is more emotional than rational—and that the thinner, lighter, faster iPad 2 transforms the original experience into something even more compelling.

In this book, I'll mainly refer to the iPad 2, but almost everything I say applies to both types of iPad. Where there's a difference in the original iPad, I note it. If you have the original iPad, you can still use this book. (The original is thicker, heavier, and has no cameras, nor FaceTime; nearly everything else is the same.) Or, you can refer to the previous edition of this book, *Sams Teach Yourself iPad in 10 Minutes*.

Getting the most out of the iPad 2 requires an active imagination, curiosity, and a willingness to try new things. That's because the iPad 2 is physically fixed—you can't add memory or other hardware to the insides—but also easily customizable by your choice of which apps to buy (where needed), download, and run out of more than 350,000 apps that are available. (About 65,000 apps are iPad-specific.)

> NOTE: **Naming of Parts**
>
> Apple refers to the new device as the iPad 2 in public statements, press releases, and so on, but the body of the device simply says iPad. Apple sometimes uses the term iPad to refer to the newer device, sometimes to refer to the older one, and sometimes to describe both at once. This can be a bit confusing, because the original iPad and the new iPad 2 are different in important ways. I'll consistently refer to the newer device as the iPad 2 in this book, to avoid confusion.

Many of you not only face the challenge of getting the most out of your own iPad 2 , but also need to prepare for others to ask you for help with their own iPad-related questions. This book arms you to meet your own needs and to help out others as well.

The iPad 2 experience has seven important components:

The first is the device itself, which is almost an object of art, while serving as a compelling computing tool.

The second is the software that animates the iPad 2, the iPad, the iPhone, and iPod Touch: iOS. This operating software, originally developed for the iPhone, has scaled up well to the demands of the much larger iPad 2. (iOS works on both the iPad 2 and original iPad, but it lacks a few features, such as FaceTime, when run on the original iPad.) The iPad hardware, iOS, and apps work together to bring multi-touch interaction to a new level.

The third component of the iPad 2 experience is the apps that come with the iPad 2, plus the ones you add yourself. These allow for learning, fun, and creativity. The apps ecosystem is a welcome byproduct of the iPhone's growth, now with a new canvas, the iPad and iPad 2, which share the same large screen for developers to paint on.

The fourth part of the experience is the accessories you buy with the iPad 2 or that you pick up after purchasing the device itself. Useful for protecting, powering, connecting, or otherwise enhancing your use of the iPad 2, accessories are an important part of your purchase (and also, most likely, a big chunk of your total iPad-related investment).

The fifth part is content that you download for playback on your iPad 2. Including movies, TV shows, music, books, and more, this content takes advantage of the iPad 2 as a powerful and portable playback device. Along with accessories, content is likely to make up a big part of your iPad 2-related expenditures. You can download and use the same content, in the same way, on both types of iPad.

The sixth part is content you create using the iPad 2 and an ever-increasing number of apps. This applies more strongly to the iPad 2, which can take pictures and record video clips, than to the original iPad. But both types of iPad are increasingly being used for writing, drawing, editing photos, and more. The iPad 2, in particular, is maturing as a device for creating, not just consuming, content.

The final part of the iPad 2 and original iPad experience is the interaction you have, through software, with the Internet and the Web. Many apps are portals into different kinds of online information, presented in different ways to make it as interesting and useful as the developer can manage. Interaction with the Internet and the Web is the same on both types of iPad.

This book gives you the skills to conduct the orchestra of different elements that make up the iPad 2, to manage your own team of apps on the playing field of the iPad 2 and iOS, and to get the most out of the great resources available from the iPad 2's software and on the Internet.

About This Book

As part of the *Sams Teach Yourself in 10 Minutes* guides, this book aims to teach you the ins and outs of using the iPad2, without using a lot of precious time. (Specifics that apply only to the original iPad are noted throughout the book.) Divided into easy-to-follow lessons that you can tackle in about 10 minutes each, you learn the following iPad 2 tasks and topics:

- ▶ How to choose the iPad 2 that's right for you
- ▶ How to buy accessories for your iPad 2, now and in the future
- ▶ How to manage the settings for your iPad 2 and apps

▶ Getting online via Wi-Fi and, for iPad 2 models that support it, 3G

▶ Choosing a 3G provider and data plan

▶ Using iTunes to buy and synchronize multimedia—music, videos, movies, and more—between the computer and the iPad 2

▶ Using Safari to access the Web, working around problems

▶ Using iPhone email and Gmail, with and without a live connection

▶ Managing personal information with the Calendar, Contacts, and Notes

▶ Using maps, including the live Street View in its full-screen glory

▶ Getting full-screen iPad 2 apps, as well as iPhone-sized apps, from the App Store

▶ Getting and working with photos, movies, TV shows, and video

▶ Using iBooks and the new iBooks Store, introduced first on iPad 2

▶ Getting and playing music on iPad 2

▶ Using the iWork apps for writing presentations and working with numbers

▶ Using the front-facing camera and FaceTime for video conferencing

▶ Using the rear-facing camera for taking photos and shooting video clips

▶ Using the iPad 2 Dock, external keyboard, and other accessories

▶ Hooking up to external devices such as a camera, a presentation screen, TV, or HDTV

▶ Getting the most out of iTunes with your iPad 2

After you finish these lessons and the others in this book, you'll know all you need to know to take your iPad 2 as far as you want to go with it.

Who This Book Is For

This book is aimed at new iPad 2 users who want to get the most out of the device. This includes people with and without iPhone and iPad experience and experience with the Mac, or Windows PCs, or even lacking much experience with smartphones and computers of any type. All backgrounds and levels of experience are supported.

By providing depth along with introductory information, this book also helps you help others. New technology spreads quickly among networks of family members, friends, and co-workers. Technology depends on these informal support and recommendation networks just as much as it depends on the Internet, global positioning satellite (GPS) systems, and other technical infrastructure.

The iPad family will take a long time to reach full adoption, and the picture will be muddied for iPad customers by the introduction of competing devices with some similar and some different functionality. By giving you a solid grasp of the iPad family right from the beginning, the book will not only help you, but will give you the answers when others want help getting the most out of their own iPads.

Each lesson focuses on one specific topic, such as getting the settings right for your iPad or getting online via Wi-Fi or 3G. You can skip from one topic to another, read the book through from start to finish, or both. You can also hand it to a friend, family member, or colleague so they can find the answer to a specific question.

What Do I Need to Use This Book?

All you need to use most of this book is access to any kind of iPad. For some functions, you also need at least part-time access to the Internet via Wi-Fi or 3G. For videoconferencing using FaceTime, taking photos, and using video clips, you need the iPad 2. There is detailed coverage here of a few apps and add-ons that don't come with the iPad out of the box, including iBooks, which you have to download, and a few add-ons that cost money, such as some Apple-supplied accessories.

The idea is to help you get the most out of your purchase of an iPad 2, to know what else might be worth spending money on along with it, and to help you maximize the use of the most important paid apps and accessories if you do buy them. That way, the entire iPad world opens up to you in a way that helps you best manage your time, your energy, and your money.

Conventions Used in This Book

In addition to the text and figures in this book, you'll also encounter some special boxes labeled Tip, Note, or Caution.

> TIP: Tips offer helpful shortcuts or easier ways to do something.

> NOTE: Notes are extra bits of information related to the text that might help you expand your knowledge or understanding.

> CAUTION: Cautions are warnings or other important information you need to know about consequences of using a feature or executing a task.

Screen Captures

The figures captured for this book come from the iPad 2 or the original iPad and show the iPhone OS, apps, and screenshots from the Safari web browser. You may use different settings for the iPhone and apps, and you will probably use at least some—maybe many—different apps than those featured in this book. For any of these reasons, your screens may look somewhat different than those in the book.

The iPad's iOS software is regularly updated with minor changes or major new versions, and you may use newer versions of apps, different apps, or even a different web browser. Also keep in mind that the developers of the iPad and the apps and websites shown in this book are constantly working to improve their software, websites, and the services offered on them.

New features are added regularly to iOS, apps, and web services, and old ones change or disappear. This means the screen contents change often, so your own screens may differ from the ones shown in this book. Don't be too alarmed, however. The basics, though they are tweaked in appearance from time to time, stay mostly the same in principle and usage.

LESSON 1

Introducing iPad 2

In this lesson, you learn about the iPad 2 device—what's inside it, how to use its buttons and controls, and what you see onscreen when you first start it.

The iPad 2 Inside and Out

"A thing of beauty is a joy forever," wrote John Keats, and the iPad 2 is truly a beautiful thing. Its thinness, clean lines, simple design, and very small number of visible controls makes it seem useful and friendly.

Holding it in your hands just feels right. And that's important, because you're constantly holding your iPad much of the time when you're using it. The iPad 2, even more than the original iPad, is a delight to hold and to interact with. A big reason is the thickness—or, perhaps that should be thinness, of the iPad 2. At just one-third of an inch thick, it feels thinner than it "should" be, in a good way.

It's also a delight to buy. The most bare-bones model, with 16GB of flash memory and Wi-Fi only—no 3G cellular service—is $499. This is, incredibly, less expensive than less popular, less elegant competitors with fewer apps available. Even the most expensive iPad, with 64GB of flash memory and Wi-Fi plus 3G cellular connectivity, is "only" $829—right in there with competing devices that have similar specifications.

Eventually, though, the thrill of buying the iPad, as well as the thrill of holding it, diminishes, and you start focusing more on getting stuff done. To get the most out of your iPad 2, you should understand the function of every button and control that it has, and know something about the insides as well. What the iPad 2 *doesn't* have, compared to a full personal computer, is just as important as what it *does* have.

iPad 2 Size, Weight, and Specifications

The original iPad was very thin and light for all that it did. The iPad 2, shown in Figure 1.1, is amazingly thin, and even lighter than its predecessor.

FIGURE 1.1   The iPad 2 is lovely and compact.

The iPad 2 is only about a third of an inch thick, which is about one-third thinner than the original iPad. This is enough to make a big difference in look and feel. Competing devices are not even as thin as the original iPad, and the iPad 2 makes the competition look chunky indeed.

Also, with the original iPad, the back of the device is curved, making it unsteady when resting flat on a table. The device also felt a bit heavy, and together the width, curvature, and weight made the device feel like it wanted to slide out of your hands and crash to the floor.

The iPad 2 is much flatter, making it more stable when resting on a flat surface. It rests comfortably in one or two hands and no longer feels like it wants to crash to the floor.

The iPad 2 is sized a lot like a pad of letter-size paper: 9×12" tall and just under 7×12" wide. Its thickness, only a third of an inch, is about the same as a pad of paper. The iPad 2 weighs just 1.3 pounds—half of a typical netbook's weight—and only a third or a quarter the weight of a typical notebook computer.

The size and weight of the iPad 2 are directly relevant to how you'll use it. In terms of size, carrying the iPad is easier even than carrying around a paper notebook, and in terms of weight, the iPad is only a little heavier. You may not want to carry it in a way that's visible to others because of the danger of theft, but the iPad 2 slips easily into a large purse or a small carrying case.

> NOTE: **A Margin for Error?**
> The screen display that you see when you turn on the device does-n't, unfortunately, fill the entire front of the device; it has a border of about three-fourths of an inch all around. Perhaps a future version of the iPad will fill in some or all of that margin, as has occurred with successive generations of Apple laptops.

The iPad 2's screen is 9.7" diagonally and has 1024×768 resolution in landscape mode. The original iPad has the same screen size and resolution. The iPad 2 screen works equally well in landscape or portrait mode, and the operating software switches modes for you as you turn it. You can never turn it the wrong way, although you might occasionally have a hard time finding just where the Home button is.

> NOTE: **Comparing the iPad 2 Screen to a Laptop**
> The 1024×768 resolution figure is an old computer spec; the original PCs had 640×480 resolution, the next generation was 800×600, and 1024×768 was a technical breakthrough when it followed as the third wave. Computers now support a variety of screen resolutions. A typical widescreen laptop today has screen resolution of 1280×800, much wider than the two types of iPad, and about one-third larger in total resolution.

The proportions of the iPad 2's screen are not quite those of a widescreen device, so some fully widescreen content, such as many movies or TV shows, is letterboxed—shown with blank strips of blackness above and below. Other content is shown with full vertical resolution (full height) and with a bit of the image cut off on each end, which is not usually a problem in terms of enjoying the content.

The iPad 2's screen resolution is 132 pixels per inch, a bit denser than a typical computer screen. If you own a newer iPhone with Apple's high-resolution Retina Display, you'll notice that the iPad 2 does not have a Retina Display of its own. (If it did, the iPad 2 might run slower, or be more expensive because of the additional hardware required, or both.) That might change in a future version of the iPad. The iPad 2 screen is fingerprint-resistant and pretty much spill proof, but you'll want to be careful not to scratch it, and to have a good glasses cleaning cloth or cleaning kit to keep it as shiny as when it was new.

> NOTE: **Consider Protecting Your Screen**
>
> One accessory you may want to consider for your iPad 2 is a screen protector film. It protects the screen and doesn't seem to detract from the touch sensitivity or brightness much. If you're uncertain, consider visiting a shop to see if you can try an iPad 2 with a screen protector applied.

iPad 2 Buttons and Controls

The iPad 2 has 10 buttons, controls, connectors, and input/output ports. (Eleven for the AT&T Wi-Fi+3G models, which add a tray for a micro-SIM card.) Look closely at your iPad 2 to see them—three on the top edge, one at the bottom of the screen, two on the right edge, and two on the bottom edge. Here's a brief description of each, and what it does for you:

▶ **Home button** (bottom center of screen, in portrait mode)—The Home button always takes you back to the Home screen. Double-pressing it brings up a scrollable list of currently open applications. As on the iPhone, the Home button is an important key to the iPad's simplicity and usefulness.

▶ **Front-facing camera** (center top of screen, in portrait mode)—The front-facing camera is a lower-resolution, VGA-quality camera, suitable for use with FaceTime (see Chapter 10). It's only about 0.3 megapixels, best suited for video phone calls and videoconferences. It captures and sends up to 30 frames per second.

▶ **Rear-facing camera** (top-left corner, viewing the iPad 2 from the back)—The rear-facing camera is a low-resolution camera, with a bit less than 1 megapixel of resolution—not even close to the 5 megapixel camera in the iPhone 4, for example. The rear-facing camera has 5x digital zoom and captures HD-quality video (720p), up to 30 frames per second. Like the front-facing camera, the rear-facing camera lacks a flash.

▶ **Sleep/Wake button** (top-right edge)—Neither the iPad nor the iPad 2 has any moving parts, so there's nothing to start or stop. If you press it briefly, the Sleep/Wake button instantly takes the iPad from an almost no-power mode, with the screen completely off, to powered up, or vice versa. If you press it for longer, the Sleep/Wake button turns the iPad on and off.

▶ **Microphone** (top-center edge)—A tiny hole, as on many phones.

▶ **Headphone jack** (top-left edge)—A larger hole for a 3.5mm headphone jack. Many headphones you might have lying around will fit this.

▶ **Screen rotation block** (top-right edge)—A switch that can do either of two things. The original purpose is to keep the screen from re-orienting when you turn the iPad around. This is great for avoiding vertigo from the screen spinning about when you're reading in bed or laying the iPad flat on a desk. The same switch can instead be used as a Mute button for sound; you specify what the switch does in the iPad's Settings area, as described in Lesson 5, "Customizing General Settings for Your iPad."

▶ **Volume up/down** (top-right edge)—A rocker switch that does what it says on the tin. Press the top part (near the corner of the iPad's edges) to turn up the volume, and press the lower part (away from the corner) to turn down the volume.

▶ **Speaker grill** (bottom-right edge)—The speaker opening is a grill on the lower-right edge of the iPad 2; it gives surprisingly good sound.

▶ **30-pin dock connector** (bottom edge, center)—The dock connector can provide a multitude of functions. Any device that connects to it must be made by or approved by Apple, which is good
for your peace of mind (in terms of quality) and Apple's profits
(Apple charges a licensing fee for third parties who make devices
that plug into the dock connector).

The iPad 2 lacks many typical computer connectors, but most visibly and
consequentially, it lacks any USB connectors—not even one. This is a
huge source of frustration to the computer-oriented press, and also to many
users who have invested a lot in various USB-connected devices, such as a
mouse (for a humble example), a camera (you need Apple's Camera
Connection Kit, described later in this lesson), or a printer (you can only
use a few AirPrint-ready printers, all of which are from HP at this writing).
However, Apple's tight control of peripherals, and specifically not including a USB connector, does contribute to the overall high quality of the
iPad and its ecosystem of hardware and software.

Using iPad 2 Controls

Using the controls for the iPad 2 is simple. You can lock it, turn it on or
off, and even capture a screen image.

The iPad has a sleep state and a fully off state. In the sleep state, it powers
partway down very quickly, uses very little power—it takes a month to
drain the battery from a full charge in the sleep state—and comes back on
very quickly. (Going to sleep and waking each takes less than a second.)

In the fully off state, the iPad 2 uses no power at all, although the battery
might discharge very gradually over many months.

When the iPad 2 first comes back on, whether from being in sleep mode or
being turned off, it goes into a locked mode (see Figure 1.2). That means
the iPad 2 is insensitive to any input except your finger dragging a slider
about 2" from left to right. If you don't unlock the screen fairly quickly—
within about 5 seconds—the device goes back to sleep. This is to prevent
accidentally turning on the device into full-power mode and draining the
battery. This is also where you'll see the password entry screen if you
choose to use password protection as well. (See Lesson 3, "Editing Text
and Using Multi-Touch," for the relevant settings.)

FIGURE 1.2 The iPad 2 needs your help to fully awaken.

Table 1.1 shows how to use the iPad 2's controls to manage the device.

TABLE 1.1 Using the iPad 2's Controls to Get Things Done

Task	Steps
Turn iPad 2 off	Hold down the Power button for about three seconds, which brings up a red slider at the top of the screen. Slide the slider across the screen to complete turning the iPad 2 fully off.
Put iPad 2 to sleep	Press and release the Power button, but do not hold it down.
Turn iPad 2 on after sleep	Hold down the Power button briefly, which brings up a gray slider at the bottom of the screen. Slide the slider across the screen to complete turning the iPad 2 fully on.

TABLE 1.1   Using the iPad 2's Controls to Get Things Done

Task	Steps
Turn iPad 2 on after power-off	Hold down the Power button briefly, but longer than for turning on the iPad 2 after sleep—about a full second. (A brief touch of the Power button, when the iPad 2 is fully off, has no effect.) The Apple icon will display for about 10 seconds, and then a gray slider appears at the bottom of the screen. Slide the slider across the screen to complete turning the iPad 2 fully on.
Stop screen image from rotating	Get the iPad 2 screen in the desired orientation; then slide the screen rotation lock down. (If the switch is configured this way rather than as a volume mute switch; see Chapter 5.)
Allow screen image to rotate	Slide the screen rotation lock up.
Change volume	Press the Volume Up or Volume Down button. Mute is achieved by continuing to hold the Power Down button until the volume is zero. (Mute can also be enabled by using the switch that otherwise serves as the screen rotation lock; see Chapter 5.)
Return to Home screen	Press the Home button.
Take a screenshot	To capture the current screen image, press the On/Off button and then quickly press the Home button. There will be a white flash and a click, and the current screen image will be saved into the Photo application.
Bring up the task list	To bring up the list of currently running tasks, double-press the Home button.

Inside the iPad 2

The most important thing about the inside of the iPad 2 is that you're never supposed to need to see it. The iPad is not user-openable or upgradable; if you try to open it, you not only void the warranty, you risk breaking the device so it won't close up again—an unnecessary waste of the hundreds of dollars that you spent to buy your iPad 2.

The inside of the iPad 2 contains several elements worthy of note, as follows:

- **A5 processor**—The dual-core A5 central processing unit is designed by a team at Apple. The A5 processor runs at up to 1GHz, which is very fast compared to most smartphones, but slower than a personal computer. The A5 processor controls graphics as well as standard computer processing, and it is thought to be carefully engineered for power management and cool operation.

- **512MB of RAM**—A processor such as the A5 uses RAM as working storage for code and data that it's currently processing. The iPad 2 has a moderate amount of RAM, which is enough to get the job done, but small enough to force software developers to manage their programs' RAM usage carefully.

- **16GB, 32GB, or 64GB of flash memory**—Instead of a hard disk, Apple provides storage as solid-state memory with no moving parts. The amount of flash memory most directly affects how much music and video you can store on the device, as well as the price (about $100 for each step up in flash memory size).

- **Wi-Fi and, optionally, 3G hardware**—All iPad 2 units have Wi-Fi built in, but only some have 3G for cellular network access, and then only at a price (about $130 extra at launch). 3G hardware is helpful for location and navigation services as well as for data transfer in more locations.

- **Three batteries**—Three batteries—about the height and width of a deck of playing cards, but thinner—occupy almost all the height and width and about half the depth of the iPad. They provide a total of about 25 watt-hours of power.

▶ **Three-axis gyroscope and accelerometer**—These devices let
the iPad 2 know where it's positioned and how fast it's moving
through space. The iPad 2 also includes a digital compass to help
with location. Together, they make up a powerful combination for
navigation and, especially, games.

TIP: **Keeping Your iPad 2 Going**

The best way to keep your iPad 2 running for a long time when it's
not plugged in and charging is to turn down the screen brightness
as low as possible. The trick is to remember to turn down the
brightness at the beginning of a session and again whenever a
change in the ambient lighting makes it possible. If you wait to turn
down the screen brightness until you're almost out of power, it will
be too late to make much of a difference.

The system performance of the components of the iPad and iPad 2 has
amazed even hardened computer and smartphone reviewers. They note, with
approval, that the iPad and iPad 2 both last even longer than the 10 hours
that Apple claims for just about any normal operations, such as watching
video, using apps, surfing the Web, and so on.

You may wonder about the difference in specifications between the iPad 2
and the original iPad. The iPad 2 is a solid upgrade, based on technical
specifications:

▶ The A5 processor in the iPad 2 is dual-core, whereas the A4
processor in the original iPad is single core. Both run at 1GHz,
but the two cores in the A5 processor mean that operations run
up to twice as fast. Graphics support in the A5 is also improved
over the A4, with Apple claiming an overall improvement of up
to nine times faster.

▶ The 512MB of RAM in the iPad 2 is double the 256MB of RAM
in the original iPad, which is very good for system speed, especially graphics speed.

▶ Flash memory amounts—and the prices associated with having
more flash memory—are the same for the iPad 2 as they were for
the original iPad.

▶ The Wi-Fi hardware in the iPad 2 is the same as in the original iPad.

▶ The 3G hardware in the iPad 2 is more flexible, allowing the device to be configured to run on either a CDMA cellular network (like Verizon) or a GSM network (like AT&T). This configuration is performed by a vendor, not by you.

▶ The three batteries in the iPad 2, which provide its amazing 10-hour battery life, are smaller in total size than the two batteries in the original iPad, but have just a little bit more capacity—the equivalent of a few minutes' worth of running time.

▶ The three-axis gyroscope in the iPad 2 makes the device "smarter" about its position in space.

NOTE: **Why iPad 2 Lasts So Long**

The hard disk uses a lot of the power budget on laptop computers and netbooks. In fact, these devices will typically spin down or "rest" the hard disk frequently, which saves power but means that you sometimes have to wait a moment while the device spins back up. The USB port also draws power to supply devices connected to it. A big advantage of the iPad 2, in terms of power consumption, is that it doesn't have either of these energy-draining components.

---

iPad 2 Accessories

The iPad 2 has many kinds of accessories. It's good to know the main classes of accessories in order to know just how you can extend the usefulness of your iPad.

There are three types of accessories I'll mention here: accessories included with the iPad 2, accessories sold under the Apple brand, and third-party accessories.

NOTE: **Finding a Lost or Stolen iPad 2**

Apple has created a useful app for finding a lost or stolen iPad 2, or any other iOS device. You should download it and set it up early

---

in your time as an iPad 2 owner so you can easily continue owning
your iPad 2! See Lesson 12, "Getting Apps from the App Store," for
details.

Accessories Included with the iPad

The iPad includes a 10W USB power adapter and a dock connector to
USB cable. The 10W USB power adapter plugs into a socket. The cable
plugs into the socket (on the USB end) and the iPad (on the dock connector end). This powers the device. The iPad takes a few hours to recharge.

You can also recharge the iPad 2 by plugging the USB end of the power
adapter into some computer USB sockets. All Macs have the appropriate
type of USB socket; most PCs don't. Even with the right type of USB
socket, charging the iPad from your computer takes about twice as long as
when you charge from a wall socket. Charging your iPad 2 from your laptop also drains the laptop's batteries if it's not plugged in. It's better to
think of this as something you do in a pinch than as a standard way to
charge your iPad.

The iPad-to-computer USB connection is also useful for transferring
data—music, movies, and more. You can also transfer media wirelessly, as
explained in Lesson 18, "Using iTunes and Home Sharing," Check to see
how quickly your iPad recharges when plugged in for this purpose, so you
know what to expect if you want or need to do it this way.

You'll probably want more accessories. For instance, protecting the iPad's
lovely finish and its screen have to be priorities. On the other hand, Steve
Jobs once said that the scratches and dings on his iPhone were a form of
weathering that made the device more attractive, not less, so everyone's
needs are different. That's why most accessories are optional—and why
picking them out is so much fun.

Accessories Available from Apple

Apple offers a number of accessories with the iPad—some are "must
haves," some should be considered along with third-party alternatives, and
others are specialist tools.

Here's a brief rundown of the major types of accessories that Apple has an entry for, and a description of Apple's product, or products, in each. For alternatives, check online (Apple's site is Apple only), in a physical Apple store (with both Apple and third-party products), and in other stores that carry electronic products (often including third-party products, but few Apple products).

iPad Smart Cover

Apple has designed a new kind of cover called a Smart Cover, which is shown in Figure 1.3. The Smart Cover works only with the iPad 2, not the original iPad. Although it's an accessory costing either $69 for the leather version or $39 for neoprene, it's gotten as much positive attention as many of the built-in features of the iPad 2. And it really is pretty darn cool.

FIGURE 1.3   The iPad 2 Smart Cover.

It's hard to describe what the Smart Cover looks like, or how it works, until you see it in action. The Smart Cover is made up of four connected slats. You unroll it into a flat surface to cover the face of the iPad; it locks easily into place using magnets built into the iPad 2. When you don't need to cover your iPad, you roll it into a kind of triangular stand that supports the iPad 2 in either portrait or landscape mode.

Unlike the iPad Cover that Apple introduced for the iPad, the Smart Cover leaves the back and edges of the device exposed. This makes it likely that the surface will be nicked and scratched, which is ugly to some, but—as Steve Jobs put it—weathered to others. It would seem that Apple wants to give you the ability to be very casual indeed with your iPad, covering the glass with the Smart Cover, then tossing it into a bag, handbag, backpack, and so on with little thought as to its safety.

Smart Covers come in many colors: five color choices for leather, including a Product*Red option that supports charitable causes, and five different color choices for neoprene.

> NOTE: **Getting Your iPad 2 Engraved**
>
> For online orders only, you can get your iPad 2 engraved with a gift message, name, phone number, or whatever you please. Consider ordering online if you want your iPad 2 engraved.

There are bound to be many other cases for iPad, and some may be different in ways that make them a better fit for you or better for use in some situations. However, because of its flexibility and innovativeness, many will consider Apple's Smart Cover to be pretty much a must have. Others will want a cover that wraps around the entire device for use in at least some situations.

Docks and Keyboards

You will almost certainly want a dock for your iPad 2. The dock is a charging stand that holds the iPad 2 nearly straight, but tilted back at a slight angle so you can use it fairly easily while charging it or keeping it charged.

The dock has a plug for the dock connector to USB cable that comes with the iPad, which you can use to connect to a charger for recharging or to a computer for data transfer and, for computers that support it, recharging. The other connect is an audio line-out port to connect speakers to sound coming from your iPad. (The audio cable you need for this is sold separately.)

You also have the option of buying Apple's wireless keyboard. It's a slender, single piece of aluminum, with a rolled edge at the top that holds batteries and gives it a bit of altitude. The wireless keyboard (shown in Figure 1.4) connects to your iPad using Bluetooth. Just about any Bluetooth-compatible wireless keyboard will work as well.

The prices, at this writing, are $29 for the standalone dock and $69 for the standalone keyboard shown in Figure 1.4.

Apple Digital AV Adapter

Put your slides, movies, photos, and everything else that fills your iPad screen on an even bigger screen — your HDTV. The new Apple Digital AV Adapter mirrors exactly what you see on your iPad so that everyone in the room can enjoy it on your widescreen TV, video projection screen, or other HDMI-compatible display. It even routes digital audio to screens that support it. And a second built-in 30-pin connector lets you charge your iPad while it's mirroring. So you don't have to worry about running out of battery mid-meeting, mid-scene, or mid-trip down memory lane.
Learn more about Video Mirroring ›
Buy now ›

iPad Camera Connection Kit

Shoot. Connect. Enjoy. The iPad Camera Connection Kit gives you two ways to import photos and videos from a digital camera: using your camera's USB cable or directly from an SD card. iPad supports standard photo formats, including JPEG and RAW, as well as SD and HD video formats, including H.264 and MPEG-4. So you can get photos and videos off your camera and onto your iPad — moments after you take them.
Buy now ›

Camera Connector   SD Card Reader

FIGURE 1.4 The iPad 2 dock and keyboard from Apple.

With the standalone keyboard, you can sit back in a chair and type at your iPad a few feet away, and you can carry around the keyboard and the iPad, without needing the dock, to go mobile.

People swear by them, but having a keyboard, no matter how gorgeous, with your iPad still seems a bit odd. The keyboard does make entering text much easier, but it takes your hands away from the iPad's touchscreen. There's no mouse, so to move the cursor around onscreen, you have to touch the screen. Selecting is quite tricky, and you may find yourself setting down the keyboard, selecting text by touching the screen with your finger, and then returning everything back to normal. It's common to hear of people getting a keyboard to use with their iPad and then never using the keyboard.

The bottom line is that the keyboard is quite useful sometimes, but it doesn't make an iPad into a full personal computer—they're still quite different.

Power and Connector Cables

Apple sells power and connector cables for the iPad, as follows:

- ▶ **Apple Digital AV Adapter**—Easy HD video output, via HDMI, to a monitor, TV, and so on. With the iPad 2, the image on the external device can be an exact mirror of the image on the iPad 2's screen—or, alternatively, video output specified by the currently running app. Price: $39.

- ▶ **Camera Connection Kit**—Lets you send photos directly from a camera's USB port or directly from an SD card, without using a computer as an intermediary. It's great if you take many pictures, and it lets you use the iPad and its Wi-Fi and/or 3G wireless connection to transmit photos to others on the go. Price: $29. The Digital AV Adapter and the Camera Connection Kit are shown in Figure 1.5.

- ▶ **10W USB Power Adapter with 6' cord**—A suitable replacement for, or addition to, the 10W USB Power Adapter with a too-short 3' cord that Apple includes with the iPad. If you buy the new one with the longer cord, you can use the old one with the shorter cord as a travel kit. Price: $29.

▶ **iPad VGA Adapter**—VGA input to a monitor, TV, and so on. Price: $29.

▶ **Apple Composite AV Cable and Apple Component AV Cable**— If you want to send both streaming video and full stereo sound to a big-screen TV, you need one of these cables, depending on which works with your big-screen TV. The cables include composite or component video connectors, audio, and USB connectors. Price: $39 for either. The power adapter cord, VGA adapter, and AV cables are shown in Figure 1.6.

iPad 2 Dock

This sleek dock stand is your personal hub for all things iPad. Get easy access to a port for syncing or charging, and an audio line out port for connecting to powered speakers via an optional audio cable. The iPad 2 Dock also supports other iPad accessories, such as the Apple Digital AV Adapter and the iPad Camera Connection Kit.

Buy now ▸

Apple Wireless Keyboard

The incredibly thin Apple Wireless Keyboard uses Bluetooth technology, which makes it compatible with iPad. And you're free to type wherever you like — with the keyboard in front of your iPad or on your lap.

Buy now ▸

FIGURE 1.5 Apple's AV adapter and camera connection kit.

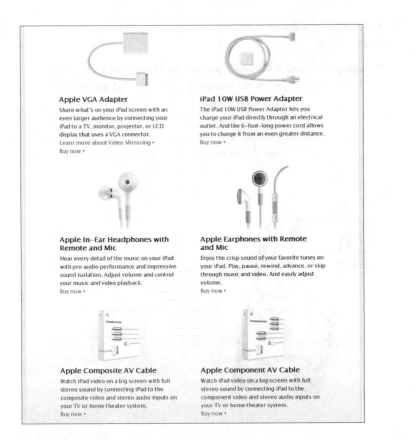

Apple VGA Adapter
Share what's on your iPad screen with an even larger audience by connecting your iPad to a TV, monitor, projector, or LCD display that uses a VGA connector.
Learn more about Video Mirroring ›
Buy now ›

iPad 10W USB Power Adapter
The iPad 10W USB Power Adapter lets you charge your iPad directly through an electrical outlet. And the 6-foot-long power cord allows you to charge it from an even greater distance.
Buy now ›

Apple In-Ear Headphones with Remote and Mic
Hear every detail of the music on your iPad with pro audio performance and impressive sound isolation. Adjust volume and control your music and video playback.
Buy now ›

Apple Earphones with Remote and Mic
Enjoy the crisp sound of your favorite tunes on your iPad. Play, pause, rewind, advance, or skip through music and video. And easily adjust volume.
Buy now ›

Apple Composite AV Cable
Watch iPad video on a big screen with full stereo sound by connecting iPad to the composite video and stereo audio inputs on your TV or home theater system.
Buy now ›

Apple Component AV Cable
Watch iPad video on a big screen with full stereo sound by connecting iPad to the component video and stereo audio inputs on your TV or home theater system.
Buy now ›

FIGURE 1.6   Apple's power, VGA, and AV cables.

CAUTION: **Check Electrical Licenses**

Don't use unlicensed third-party electronics products with your iPad, due to the potential electrical and fire dangers of anything electronic that doesn't meet all applicable standards.

These power and connector cables are all perfectly adequate. However, anytime you see a bunch of different things priced the same, you suspect that at least some of them might actually be available for less. You may want to shop around to check out competitors for some of these products, to the extent that Apple allows them to exist by granting licenses for them.

Earphones and Headphones

Earphones and headphones are very much an item of personal taste—and something that is likely to require a personal trial as well. Unless you're in a big hurry to get this part of your iPad-related shopping over with, consider going to an Apple store or other store and trying out some different headphones before committing.

Apple offers two kinds of earphones for the iPad:

▶ **Earphones with Remote and Mic**—This is a very phone-like pair of earphones with a remote control and microphone on the cable, at a low price. Price: $29.

▶ **In-Ear Headphones with Remote and Mic**—These go in your ear, just like earphones; the name In-Ear Headphones is meant to imply higher quality than plain old earphones. Experts say that you can get a lot more enjoyment from music by upgrading your earphones or headphones just a little bit, and this is Apple's bid to sell you the recommended upgrade. Price: $79.

Apple has put together a couple of credible offerings here by having two products originally created for the iPhone. This is the one item, however, that you're almost sure to want to shop for in person, so you can try competing Apple and third-party products at various price levels before deciding.

You can easily find very inexpensive and very fancy earphones, noise-canceling headphones, clever on-ear and around-ear headphones, and much more. It's worth checking out these products in person before buying.

Third-Party Accessories

The iPod music player and the iPhone have incited a tidal wave of accessories, and the iPad is no different. Here are some of the major categories of accessories to consider if you are ready to go shopping, online or in person:

▶ **Adapters and chargers**—Power adapters like the ones Apple offers, plus adapters for cars, and many others as well.

▶ **Batteries**—The iPad 2's 10-hour charge reduces the need for an add-on battery, but there will always be people who need more than the included amount of portable power. Add-on batteries plug in to keep your iPad going when it's otherwise out of power, but of course they add weight and bulk to what you have to carry.

▶ **Cases and skins**—Every material, thickness, color, and degree of protection you can imagine has been, or probably will be, made for the iPad 2. Be sure not to buy something sized for the original iPad, which is about 50% thicker.

▶ **Cables**—Longer and different kinds of charging and data transfer cables.

▶ **Earphones and headsets**—Every taste and budget accounted for.

▶ **Keyboards**—Foldable, slimmer, and less-expensive alternatives to Apple's aluminum marvel.

▶ **Printers**—The iPad 2, and all iOS devices, support AirPlay, which lets you print directly to a limited number of HP printers that are advertised as AirPlay-ready.

▶ **Screen protectors**—Many different screen protective films, pre-cut to fit the iPad 2.

▶ **Speakers**—You can make your own home stereo system based around your iPad 2.

▶ **Stylus pens**—Use a special stylus instead of a finger for more accurate and quicker data entry.

The possibilities, within these categories and in addition to them, are almost endless. For instance, if your iPad is feeding your TV or stereo, can a remote control for it be far behind? Use your imagination to come up with a new idea today, and you'll probably see it in the iPad store tomorrow.

Summary

In this lesson, you learned about the specifications of the iPad 2 and what they mean for using it, the iPad 2's hardware controls and how to use them, what's inside the iPad 2, and the Apple accessories available for it. In the next lesson, you'll find out how to set up and work with the iPad 2's Home screen features.

LESSON 2

Setting Up and Us
the Home Screen

In this lesson, you learn your way around the iPad 2 Home screen—what
on it, what all the little symbols in the status bar and changes in them
mean, and how to customize the app layout onscreen. You also learn how
to search data you've entered across your iPad's apps.

The iPad's Touchscreen

Apple had a huge success with the Macintosh, beginning in 1984, largely
as the result of the Mac's fully integrated use of a relatively new invention:
the computer mouse. On the Mac, the mouse was used to do amazing
things, such as driving the interface to professional-level drawing and
video-editing applications on an affordable personal computer.

Apple then recognized touch as the next big thing in computer interfaces
and started working to further embrace and extend its use. The first big
step was the integration of multi-touch capabilities as the main interaction
tool for iPod music players and the iPhone. This technology has also been
integrated into the trackpads for Mac portables, where multi-finger gestures control a variety of user interactions.

The iPad 2 is the next logical evolution in the use of touch, and it repre-
sents a giant step forward. Being able to view personal computer-type content and tools and interact with them via touch, on a nearly full-size computer screen that you hold in your hands, is instantly understood as a
breakthrough by nearly everyone who tries using an iPad 2. The same goes
for having a video conference call over a handheld device and being able
to modify how people are presented onscreen with the touch of a finger.

The iPad 2 screen is a rich, responsive, and wonderful thing—engineered,
in hardware and software, to be as touch friendly as any computing device

e most out of it, you should understand some of the
ever made it works.
details o

Stа icons

The bar—the thin black bar across the top of the iPad screen—is the
The de for communication about the state of your iPad. Some apps
ma t in place; others, particularly games, take up every pixel of the
le en, covering up the status bar. It's a bit disconcerting when an app cov-
s up the status bar.

The status bar is like a bulletin board for messages from the iPad to you.
Being able to quickly scan and understand what you do—and don't—see
in the status bar as you use your iPad will help you get a lot more out of it.

There are several types of status icons. Details for the settings that help
you control each type of icon are given in later lessons. Following are the
icons themselves and what they mean to you.

Wireless Communications Icons

Bluetooth is a protocol for transferring data between devices near each
other. You should turn on Bluetooth when needed, such as when you're
about to use a wireless keyboard. You should turn off Bluetooth at other
times, because it uses power and can be used to try to steal information off
your computer when you're out and about.

To turn Bluetooth on or off, press Settings, General, then press Bluetooth,
and use the slider to toggle it on or off.

There are four possible ways for an iPad 2 to transfer data over the
Internet: Wi-Fi, available on all iPads, is the first. There are then three progressively faster and more capable types of data transfer over a cellphone
wireless network: GPRS (also known as 2G), EDGE (also known as
2.5G), and 3G. These latter three types of data transfer are available only
on iPad 2 Wi-Fi+3G models, and only function when you activate a wireless data plan with a provider.

> TIP: **Free or Inexpensive 4G for Any iPad**
> There were some complaints at the launch of the iPad 2 that 4G
> support wasn't included in the device. However, you can get 4G-

type performance for any iPad or iPad 2, even t.
Just get a phone that has 4G support and the ab.. ones.
portable Wi-Fi hotspot. Hotspot support is free on .ate a
phones, while one iPhone provider currently charges .roid
for it. The iPhone supports this capability, calling it P. .onth
HotSpot; it's currently $20 a month from one provider. .an.
Android phones offer the capability for free. So when 4. vers.
of these phones come out, you can use them to pover .porta..
hotspot. You can then connect to this 4G-powered hots.. from
your iPad or iPad 2 and share the connection with up to .ur other
laptops, netbooks, tablets, and so on.

Also available only on iPad 2 Wi-Fi+3G models is Airplane mode, which turns off all Internet access and Bluetooth. If you're on an airplane with a non-3G iPad 2, you'll need to turn off Wi-Fi (so your iPad won't search for a network) and Bluetooth directly.

The activity icon displays network activity, such as refreshing a web page, and some other activity as well. It's used as an indicator by third-party applications to show they're working.

The VPN icon shows if you're connected to a virtual private network. This is usually applicable only if you have the okay to use your iPad 2 for work or school and are accessing your organization's servers via your iPad.

To sum up, at any given time, you'll see up to four icons for wireless communication on a Wi-Fi-only iPad, and up to two out of four further icons showing for your 3G connection:

▶ Bluetooth, if Bluetooth is available for connections. (Turn off Bluetooth when you aren't specifically using it, for security reasons and to save a bit of battery life.)

▶ Wi-Fi (also shows connection strength), if you're connected to a Wi-Fi network.

▶ VPN, if you're connected to a virtual private network.

▶ Activity, for network and some other kinds of activity.

▶ iPad Wi-Fi+3G only: GPRS, EDGE, 3G, or Airplane mode, if you either are connected to a cellular wireless network (GPRS,

EDG   d 3G)   ve turned off all forms of wireless access
fro   G iPa   Airplane mode).

In Airp mode   detooth, Wi-Fi, and cellular wireless are shut off. If
you're   an airp   e with a Wi-Fi-only iPad, just turn off Bluetooth and
Wi-F

ner Icons

ost of the p   sible icons in the status bar relate to wireless communication. There e only four others:

▶ **Battery**—Shows the current battery charging level and charging
  status. (The battery icon shows a plug icon when plugged in, no
  icon when not.)

▶ **Play**—A song, audiobook, or podcast is playing. See Lesson 16,
  "Using iPad 2 for Music and More," and Lesson 17, "Using
  iBooks and the iBookstore," for details.

▶ **Lock**—Shows that the screen is locked. You'll already know this
  because the iPad will be displaying the unlock screen.

▶ **Screen rotation lock**—Shows that the screen rotation lock is on.

Included Apps

If apps are the secret of getting the most out of the iPad 2, the included
apps are "the secret of the secret." New, exciting apps that become available through the App Store seem to get all the attention, whether free or
downloaded. Yet many people don't spend enough time using the included
apps to full advantage. People repeatedly chase new apps when the ones
that everyone already has can get an awful lot of the things you need done.

Dock Apps

There are four apps in the Dock, the bottom bar of the iPad 2 Home
screen. Not only is the Dock available on the first pane of the Home
screen; it's available on every pane.

These key apps are as follows:

▶ **Safari**—This is the built-in web browser for the iPad 2, and the portal to a great deal of functionality whenever you have Internet access via Wi-Fi or the cellphone wireless network. If you use a different browser—at this writing, the Terra browser and the Atomic Web browser are among the browsers available for the iPad 2—you may want to put that browser in the bottom browser bar instead.

▶ **Mail**—Apple's built-in mail. See Lesson 7, "Synching, Sending, and Receiving Email," for details.

▶ **Photos**—The Photos app is used for viewing photos that you take with your iPad 2 or import from elsewhere. You can use the Camera Connection Kit to attach a camera directly to your iPad 2 and download photos via the Web or PC, to edit them or just build up your stock on your iPad 2.

▶ **iPod**—The iPod app is the interface to music on your iPad 2. The iPad 2 is a fantastic music machine, and the iPad 2's slightly limited multitasking has strong support for playing music in the background. If you use a streaming app, or some other app for music instead of iPad 2, consider putting that other app on the bottom bar instead.

TIP: **Multitasking Still a Bit Limited**

For a long time, iOS devices—the iPod Touch, iPhone, and the iPad—didn't support multitasking. However, a few months before the iPad 2 came out, Apple updated iOS to include a limited form of multitasking. So, the iPad 2 has always had this capability. iOS makes certain background services, such as playing music, available to apps. However, some multitasking that takes place on a personal computer—such as downloading a web page in the background, even when it's offscreen—doesn't happen on iOS.

The bottom bar can accommodate up to six apps. Consider replacing and adding to the original four apps in the bottom bar to create a working set of the apps you use the most, and that you want available on every pane of the Home screen. Customizing the Home screen is explained later in this lesson.

> TIP: **Status and Dock Always Visible**
>
> The iPad 2 supports up to 11 separate, full-page panels for your Home screen, depending on how you arrange the Icons and folders that hang out there. The status bar at the top and the Dock of selected app icons at the bottom are always visible on all Home screens.

Home Screen Apps

The Home screen includes nine additional apps, and you may want to consider adding the iBooks app to this core group as well, to make a total of 10. Here are brief descriptions of all of them:

▶ **Calendar**—The Calendar app trades information with other calendars: Apple's iCal and MobileMe, Microsoft Entourage (Mac) and Microsoft Outlook (Windows) personal information managers, and Microsoft Exchange, commonly used by medium-sized and large organizations. (Yahoo! Calendar and Google Calendar are notable for being left out here.)

▶ **Contacts**—The Contacts app synchs with Apple's MobileMe and Mac OS X Address Book; Yahoo! Address Book and Google Contacts; and Microsoft Outlook, Microsoft Exchange, and Windows Address Book as used by Microsoft Express.

▶ **Notes**—The Notes app is highly underrated (I've even heard people complain about the font it uses). It's a free, easy-to-use tool that replaces a paper notepad and is easier to carry, along with the iPad 2, than a paper notepad (and with far more flexibility). It's also much easier to carry than a laptop, and much less obtrusive in use. It just takes one button push to send your (scrolling) page of notes out as an email message, which is highly convenient for sending out notes just after a meeting. See Lesson 8, "Using Contacts and Notes," for details.

▶ **Maps**—The Maps app, from Google, is great—it even supports Street View in glorious full-screen. However, Maps lacks

turn-by-turn directions, which are found for free on some Google
Android devices, and it doesn't work as well on a Wi-Fi-only
iPad 2 rather than an iPad 2 Wi-Fi+3G. (This is because access to
3G networks makes the GPS capability work better as well.)
Lesson 11, "Working with Maps," has more information.

► **Videos**—Plays video content—including movies, TV shows,
video podcasts, and other videos you buy on iTunes or play from
your own collection. See Lesson 15, "Playing Videos and
YouTube," for details on videos and YouTube as well.

► **YouTube**—Does what it says on the tin—a direct, full-screen
interface into YouTube and its collection of videos. You can
search or browse categories and do everything a YouTube account
will allow, such as add ratings to videos and synchronize
favorites between your iPad 2, your personal computer, and more.

► **iTunes**—Direct access to the iTunes store, which you can search
for all kinds of media, including music, audiobooks, music
videos, TV shows, movies, and more. You can then download
what you need directly to your iPad 2. As on YouTube, you can
review items. (See Lesson 5, "Customizing General Settings for
Your iPad 2.")

► **App Store**—The famous Apple App Store contains a mix of apps
totaling more than a hundred thousand, though most are not yet
iPad 2 optimized. Shopping for an app, when you don't already
know which one you want by name, can be difficult—there are
hundreds of thousands of apps in the App Store, and they are not
all that well-organized—but fun. Lesson 12, "Getting Apps from
the App Store," has details.

► **Settings**—The iPad 2 has surprisingly simple core settings for all
it does, while apps have their own settings in the Settings area as
well. Settings are covered in Lesson 5, "Customizing General
Settings for Your iPad 2," and other lessons.

► **iBooks**—iBooks is Apple's online bookstore and includes hundreds of thousands of titles, free and paid. The app doesn't show
up on the Home screen, but you should add it to other core Apple
apps (no pun intended), as described later in this lesson, as soon

as you're ready to check it out. Lesson 17, "Using iBooks and the iBookstore," has details.

▶ **FaceTime and Photobooth**—FaceTime is Apple's app for video-conferencing. It uses the front-facing camera to show your smiling face, and the rear-facing camera to allow you to show the people calling you what your surrounding environment looks like. Photo Booth applies a series of visual filters to liven up the current video image. Lesson 10, "Using FaceTime," gets specific.

▶ **Camera**—The Camera app is focused (no pun intended) on the rear-facing camera on the iPad 2. The rear-facing camera is relatively low-resolution—a mere 0.7Mpx, where 2Mpx is the bare minimum to produce a quality photograph, and 5Mpx is common on mobile phones today. See Lesson 13, "Taking Photos," for more.

▶ **Game Center**—Game Center is a light front end for games on the iPad. With the new capabilities in the iPad 2, expect some killer games that take advantage of features such as the 3-axis gyroscope and even the cameras. For more about apps in general, including games, see Lesson 12, "Getting Apps from the App Store."

One key decision to make going in is whether you're going to use the iPad 2 for personal information management, such as your contacts and the calendar. The iPad 2 is a really cool way to do this, but if you already handle it through your personal computer and/or smartphone, you may not want to do it on the iPad 2 as well.

If your smartphone is an iPhone, personal information management may more or less automatically get handled on the iPad 2 as well. Otherwise, think carefully about whether you want to handle these updates on the iPad 2 instead of, or in addition to, a smartphone, or just not bother with that on the iPad 2.

If you have an iPad 2 Wi-Fi+3G that you tend to carry around with you almost, or fully, as much as a smartphone, it might make sense to have your personal information on the iPad 2. However, your iPad 2 is not where you handle phone calls or text messages, so a key interactive function of personal information management is missing. Also, the iPad 2 is easier to type on than an iPhone, but not as easy as a laptop. The bottom line: You may not want the hassle of using personal information management apps on the iPad 2.

Using the Home Screen

The iPad 2's Home screen has several panes, areas for additional icons that you reach by swiping left or right onscreen to move left or right among the panes. The panes are home to icons for various apps—the original set that comes with your iPad 2, plus additional apps you've downloaded and installed. Apps can take their place on the Home screen with their original icons, or you can put apps into folders and give the folders descriptive or whimsical names. (Any kind of name you want, really.)

The app bar appears across the bottom of the screen and remains in place even when you change panes. When you get your iPad 2, the app bar includes the built-in Safari Web browser and the Mail, Photos, and iPod apps. However, you can change which apps are in the app bar and add up to two more apps to it for a total of six.

The Home screen also includes the following:

▶ **A Search screen**—This screen appears to the left of the core Home screen. To reach the Search screen, press the Home button to reach the core Home screen; then drag your finger horizontally, left to right, to scroll left by one pane.

▶ **The core Home screen pane**—The core Home screen is where you return when you press the Home button. This screen should have your most-used app icons to help you speedily start your most frequently used apps.

▶ **Additional Home screen panes**—As you add and move app icons to the Home screen, additional Home screen panes are added—or, when necessary, removed—to the right of the core Home screen pane. To reach them, press the Home button to return to the core Home screen, and then scroll to the right to reach the additional Home screens.

The overall Home screen expands with additional screens to fit the apps you put on it, up to a total of 11 screens with up to 20 apps each, or up to

220 apps total. (You can also put apps in folders, allowing you to have many more.)

The term *Home screen* refers to all the panes together and also to the one, single, original Home screen pane, which includes a Search screen to its left and that never goes away, even if you were to throw away all your apps.

You can think of the Home screen and its panes as being like a folding room divider with up to 11 panels, plus a search screen to the left of the first, original Home screen. Dots on every screen of the overall Home screen show how many separate screens there are, and the lit dot shows which one you're on. See Figure 2.1 for an example.

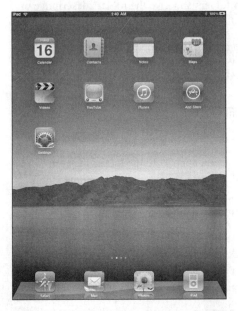

FIGURE 2.1   The Home screen includes dots that show you where you are.

Using the Home screen is easy, as follows:

▶ **Returning to the core Home screen panel**—To return to the core Home screen panel from any other iPad 2 screen, press the Home button.

▶ **Scrolling among the Home screen panels**—To scroll among the Home screen panels, just swipe horizontally from one screen to the next. Or press to the left of the row of dots to scroll one screen left; press to the right of the row of dots to scroll one screen right. To continue scrolling by an additional screen, press again.

▶ **Reaching the Search screen**—To reach the Search screen, press the Home button to return to the core Home screen; then scroll one screen to the left. (You can also press the Home button, pause briefly, then press Home again to reach the Search screen. Two quick presses brings up the task bar.)

Customizing the Home Screen

Customizing the Home screen for the iPad 2 is easy. Doing so makes your iPad 2 work the way you want it to, making it faster and simpler to get things done.

Here's what to do to customize your Home screen:

▶ **To move an app on the same screen**—Press and hold an app icon until all the app icons start shaking, and an X appears in the upper left of each icon, as shown in Figure 2.2. Drag the app icon to any spot on the screen—whether the spot is empty or occupied. The app icon will relocate to the spot you drag it to; if you've dragged it into empty space beyond other app icons, it will relocate to the first empty position.

▶ **To remove an app icon, delete the app and its data**—After you've pressed and held an app icon and started them all quivering, press the X on the upper-left corner of any app you want to remove. The app icon, the app code, and any documents and data created by the application are deleted and can't be recovered.

▶ **To update the Dock**—You can move app icons to the Dock (up to six icons), remove app icons from the Dock onto any Home screen panel, and remove app icons completely that are resident on the Dock. No matter what Home screen panel you're on when you update the Dock, after you make changes to the Dock app icons, the updated Dock appears the same on all screens.

FIGURE 2.2   Pressing one app makes them all shake.

▶ **To move an app to a new panel**—When the app icons are quivering, drag an app icon to the left or right edge of the screen. Hold it at the very edge, in a narrow region bordering the current panel and the panel that's off to the side. (This takes a bit of practice to get good at.) The panel will change from the one previously showing the icon to the new panel you targeted.

▶ **To add a panel to the Home screen (up to 11 panels total)**—If all panels are full, installing a new app (see Lesson 12, "Getting Apps from the App Store") creates a new panel, with the new app's icon on it. Also, you can add a panel by dragging an app icon beyond the right edge of the current rightmost occupied panel. You can add apps or keep dragging an icon to the right, creating new panels, for up to a total of 11 panels.

▶ **To use apps after changes**—After you've made desired changes, press the Home screen button once. The app icons will stop shaking, the X on each icon will disappear, and the number of dots shown to reflect the number of screens in the overall Home screen will update to reflect current usage.

▶ **To create and modify folders, see the next section**—Folders for app icons are a new, fun feature in iOS, added in late 2010. See the next section for instructions on how to use it. Now you know how to customize your Home screen—but how do you want it to work? You can arrange app and folder icons into sensible groups. That way, instead of finding one app icon out of as many as 220 on up to 11 screens, you first find the group of icons and/or folders you want and then the specific app icon. This can be much easier, if the groups and folders make sense.

> TIP: **Try Moving Apps**
>
> Experiment with moving apps around and creating new screens and new folders when you have a few spare minutes. That way, when you need to do it later on, it will be easy.

Think of your apps and folders as being in groups: tools, news, games, and so on. Arrange the icons into sensible groups—a row, half-screen, or full screen at a time—by theme.

There's no way to label a screen or area with a name, so the groups have to be clear and self-evident. You can put an iconic app in the upper-left corner of a group to help, such as putting a BBC News app in the upper-left corner of a group of news apps. Just having the word "News" in the app icon name BBC News will remind you what the group is about.

Creating Folders

The capability to create folders to hold apps in was added to iOS in late 2010. With folders, you not only can have a lot more apps on the Home page, you can organize them much better.

You may want to put all your apps into folders, or have the most-used apps at the top level and less-used apps in folders. It's completely up to you.

To create a folder and add apps to it, follow these steps:

1. Move apps around so that the apps you want to put into the same folder are on the same panel of the Home page.

2. Press and hold an app icon until all the icons start quivering.

3. Drag one icon on top of another. A folder containing the apps is created and given a name by iOS. The contents of the current folder display, and you can change the folder's name, as shown in Figure 2.3.

FIGURE 2.3   iOS makes creating folders easy and fun.

4. Rename the folder if you care to. Drag icons into and out of the folder until the contents are right.

5. Tap the icon for the new folder to close it.

6. Press the Home button to make the app icons stop quivering. Icons are no longer able to be dragged and dropped.

You move folders around onscreen in the same way that you do app icons, so you can arrange them on the Home screen panes as you want.

To delete a folder, drag all the apps out of it.

Switching Between Apps and Closing Apps

Apple has gradually increased the multitasking capability on the iPad 2, allowing you to have many apps at once. Every app that's running, though, takes up some of the iPad 2's RAM, which can slow the system down and increase the risk of a system crash. There are three steps you can take— one usability improvement and two maintenance steps—to improve your use of your iPad 2:

▶ Switching quickly among running apps.

▶ Closing apps you're not using.

▶ Rebooting the iPad.

The iPad 2 gives you two ways to switch among apps. To switch from one app to any other app, whether it's current or not, press the Home button. On the Home screen, you find the app you want and press the icon. The app starts; you don't really care if it was already running or not.

However, you can also switch among apps that are already running. This can be easier than finding an app on the Home screen, especially if you already have a lot of apps. Using this option can force you to spend time thinking, though, about what apps are running and which ones aren't, which does add complexity.

After you start the process of switching among apps, you can also delete any unwanted apps. If you want to take on the extra mental overhead, here's how to switch quickly among running apps and halt the ones you don't want to be running anymore:

1. Double-press the Home button.

   Doing this double-press just right can be a bit tricky, but if you do it correctly, the currently running apps appear in a strip across the bottom of your screen. If very many apps are running, the app icons scroll sideways to let you see all the apps.

2. If more than six apps are open, swipe to see more app icons off to the right.

3. To switch to an app, touch its icon.

   The app opens.

4. To turn off one or more apps, press and hold any app icon.

   The app icons all start to quiver, and a close symbol—a dash—appears on each icon, as shown in Figure 2.4.

FIGURE 2.4   Press and hold on any app to see the close symbol on all apps.

5. To close an app, press the minus sign on its icon.

The app closes. In most apps, you won't lose data. (I've noticed that a game I play, Civilization Revolution, sometimes loses a few moves of gameplay when I shut it down without saving my game and then restart.)

6. Continue closing apps until you're done.

7. To restart the iPad 2, clearing out memory completely, press the Sleep/Wake button (on the upper right of the iPad) and the Home button (on the lower-front center of the screen) at the same time.

The iPad 2 restarts.

Searching iPad 2

You can search the entire iPad 2 from the Home screen using a screen called Spotlight. Spotlight searches the data you've entered into apps, including the Notes app, Mail, Calendar, Contacts, iPod, and Video.

Here's what Spotlight searches:

▶ **Applications** –Names of all apps, whether built in or installed.

▶ **Notes**—Names of notes and note text.

▶ **Mail**—To, From, and Subject fields (but not the content of email messages) across all accounts.

▶ **Calendar**—Event titles, names of people invited, and locations.

▶ **Contacts**—First names, last names, and company names.

▶ **iPod**—Names or titles of songs, podcasts, and audiobooks, as well as artists and albums for songs.

▶ **Video**—Names of videos.

You can use Settings to change which apps are searched, and even the order in which they're searched (see Lesson 5).

With many apps, you can also search within individual apps by using Spotlight from within the app. (The developer has to implement support for Spotlight searching in the app to make it available to you. Having Spotlight search support doesn't make sense for all apps, such as many games.)

NOTE: **Don't Worry About Files on the iPad 2**

Unlike a personal computer, the iPad 2 does not have a user-accessible file system. That is, you can't get at all the files that iPhone OS, or a given app, might have. Instead, files are controlled by specific apps, which may give you access to the same files in different ways, or may not give you access to some or all files.

The whole idea of a "file" is more or less kept hidden from you. For instance, the notepad in the Notes app has many pages in it, which you can access from a scrolling list on the left (see Lesson 8). You don't ever know whether the Notes app keeps these pages as separate files or as separate parts of a single file. Part of the purpose of Spotlight is to help you get at your data, across platforms, without exposing (or making you understand and use) the file system.

To search the iPad 2, follow these steps:

1. From the Home screen, swipe sideways to scroll left to the Search screen.

2. Use the onscreen keyboard to enter the search term you want to use.

3. Press the Search button on the keypad.

   A list of search hits in various applications appears, as shown in Figure 2.5.

To search within an app, open the app and then repeat the preceding steps. The results will reflect the contents of data entered into that app only.

Changing the Brightness and Wallpaper Settings

The Brightness and Wallpaper controls are grouped together on your Settings menu because they both affect the way your iPad 2 screen looks as you're using it. The controls are shown in Figure 2.6.

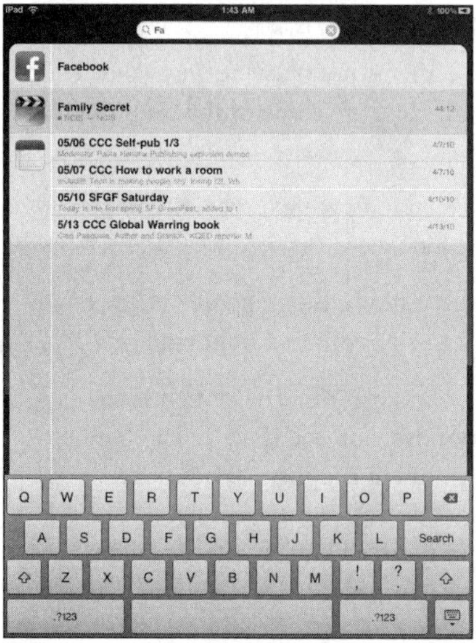

FIGURE 2.5   Searching from the Home screen gives you answers across apps.

FIGURE 2.6   Brightness and Wallpaper controls help you get the look of your iPad 2 right.

Changing Brightness Settings

The brightness of your iPad 2 screen affects not only the way your iPad 2 looks, but the way all your apps look. Here are some of the trade-offs for brightness:

- ▶ More brightness makes the screen look great, especially photos. It also seems easier to read or look at, at first.

- ▶ More brightness tires your eyes quicker. Some people have compared reading from the iPad 2 to staring into a light bulb.

- ▶ Lower brightness is better for battery life. The screen is the single biggest user of battery power on the iPad 2. The battery life of the iPad 2 is so long (rated at roughly 10 hours of continuous use) that this may not be a big concern for you, but if you find yourself running out of battery power when using your iPad 2, reducing the brightness level should make a big difference.

- ▶ Lower brightness is better for sustained reading. This is why the iBooks app, described in Lesson 15, has its own brightness control.

You're likely to do a lot of reading in other apps such as the Safari Web browser, so brightness is important no matter what you're doing with your iPad 2.

Follow these steps to change the screen brightness of your iPad 2:

1. From the Home screen, tap Settings.

2. From the Settings screen, tap Brightness and Wallpaper. The Brightness & Wallpaper settings appear.

3. To change the brightness level, drag the slider left (dimmer) or right (brighter). The screen instantly gets brighter or dimmer in response.

4. Use the Auto-Brightness slider to turn the Auto-Brightness feature on or off.

If Auto-Brightness is on, the screen will adjust, using the built-in ambient (or "surrounding") light sensor. The screen automatically dims in low light, so as to not tire your eyes, and brightens in bright light, to compete with the bright surroundings.

Changing Wallpaper Settings

Wallpaper is simply the background image on your iPad 2 screen. The image that ships on the iPad 2 before you change it is a time exposure of a meteor shower, showing the meteors as streaks across the sky. Unfortunately, the streaks can look all too much like scratches in your iPad 2 screen!

Luckily, it's easy and fun to change your wallpaper settings, choosing from the roughly 20 built-in images or any photo that you have on your iPad 2.

There are two different wallpaper choices you can make:

▶ **Lock screen**—This is the screen you see when your iPad 2 has been locked and you use the slider to unlock it.

▶ **Home screen**—This is the background for the several panes of your Home screen.

You can easily choose to use the same wallpaper on both for consistency.

Follow these steps to change the wallpaper for your iPad 2:

1. From the Home screen, tap Settings.

2. From the Settings screen, tap Brightness and Wallpaper. The Brightness & Wallpaper settings appear, including miniature versions of the current lock screen and Home screen wallpaper.

3. To change the wallpaper for the lock screen, the Home screen, or both, tap the white area under the word Wallpaper. You're given a choice of folders to choose from: a Wallpaper folder of built-in photos, plus multiple folders representing all the photos on your iPad 2.

4. Tap the folder you want to look in. A group of photos appears.

5. Tap the photo you want to inspect. The photo appears onscreen, along with buttons to use in setting the wallpaper for the two screens, as shown in Figure 2.7.

FIGURE 2.7   Choose a great photo or two for your wallpaper.

6. Tap the button Set Lock Screen to set the current photo as the lock screen photo. Tap the button Set Home Screen to set the current photo as the Home screen photo. Tap Set Both to use the current photo for both.

7. Tap Back to return to the list of folders and make further choices, or tap Home to return to the Home screen.

TIP: **Get Your Choice of Image Onscreen**
You can use any image on your iPad 2 for the lock screen and/or the Home screen wallpaper. See Lesson 14, "Importing and Viewing Photos," for details on importing photos.

Summary

In this lesson, you learned about the iPad 2's Home screen and its contents, including status bar notification icons and the Dock of app icons at the bottom. You also learned how to change the arrangement of app icons, how to use folders for apps, and how to search for data across iPad 2's apps. In the next lesson, you will learn about entering and editing text using the iPad 2's onscreen keyboard, among other options, as well as how to use the features of the multi-touch screen.

LESSON 3

Editing Text and Using Multi-Touch

In this lesson, you learn how to enter text using the iPad 2 screen, including the onscreen keyboard and the Dictionary, and how to use multi-touch on the iPad 2—the biggest multi-touch-enabled surface from Apple yet.

Entering and Editing Text

The iPad 2 is a breakthrough in many ways. Perhaps the single most important breakthrough is that it's the most ambitious attempt yet to offer computerlike functionality without a physical keyboard.

A whole raft of devices of all sizes do have physical keyboards, including laptop computers, netbooks, and the BlackBerry line of smartphones. Apple has been a real pioneer of keyboard-less devices, with the iPhone, iPod Touch, and now the iPad 2.

Even more than the iPhone, the iPad 2 and its apps are set up to reduce information entry. The device is heavily slanted toward the consumption, rather than the creation, of information. The iPad 2 system software and apps are designed to gather data from wherever they can and to reduce user input to a minimum. The challenge of entering information onto the iPad 2 is met in three ways, as follows:

▶ **Offering choices rather than typed-in information**—The iPad 2 and its apps tend to offer options and choices rather than requiring information to be typed in.

▶ **Offering onscreen keyboard(s)**—The iPad 2 offers system support for an onscreen keyboard, with options. The keyboard changes as you use it, offering portrait-mode and landscape-mode versions, different button choices for web versus other use, and so on. For instance, you will often see a key labeled .com when you are at a point in using a web browser where you are likely to enter a web URL.

▶ **Offering external keyboards**—Unlike the iPhone, the iPad 2 offers external keyboard support. Apple itself offers two keyboard options, and almost any Bluetooth keyboard works with the iPad 2.

TIP: **External Keyboard Cursor Keys**

Because the iPad 2 doesn't support a mouse, the cursor keys that you find on an external keyboard can be very useful, because they partly replace a mouse for quick and precise cursor positioning.

In this lesson, I'll emphasize typing information using the onscreen keyboard. You will need to develop onscreen keyboarding skills to get the most out of your iPad 2. However, it's good to be aware of the extent to which this requirement is reduced by software—and avoidable entirely by extra hardware, if you need it.

Using the Onscreen Keyboard

The onscreen keyboard comes up any time you need to enter text. It covers about half the screen in landscape mode, and about a third in portrait mode. In landscape mode, the onscreen keyboard is nearly as wide as a laptop's physical keyboard. However, the use of screen space by the onscreen keyboard (in either landscape or portrait mode) can interfere with your ability to see things onscreen that you need for text entry (such as when you're replying to an email).

Using the onscreen keyboard is a more interactive process than typing with a regular keyboard. The iPad 2 is constantly watching what you're typing, correcting misspellings, offering predictive suggestions for you to choose from, and learning as you use it.

The following steps show you how to successfully enter different kinds of text, as shown in Figure 3.1: upper-and lowercase letters, comma, period, exclamation point, or question mark:

FIGURE 3.1 The main onscreen keyboard.

1. To bring up the onscreen keyboard, press in a text entry area.

2. Depending on the size of your fingers, the way you are supporting the iPad 2, and your need to see text or other content onscreen, you may prefer typing in landscape mode or portrait mode. Try both, and use the one that works best for you. The portrait and landscape versions of the keyboard are identical except for the dimensions, which are larger in landscape mode.

3. To type lowercase text, a comma, or a period, press the appropriate keys on the onscreen keyboard to type. Note that, depending on the app, there may be a key with .com on it for entering URLs, or other special keys that fit the current app. Additionally, tap and hold the .com button to access the option to choose .net, .org, .us, or .edu instead.

4. To type capital letters, the ! symbol, or the ? symbol, press Shift and then the letter. Or press and hold on the Shift key, slide your finger to the letter you want, and then release your finger. Shift is retained for the last letter you touch before raising your finger.

5. Double-press the Shift key to turn it blue, meaning Caps Lock is on. To remove Caps Lock, press the Shift key once. (If Caps

Lock doesn't work for you, or to turn it off if you don't like it, see the Settings, as described in Lesson 5, "Customizing General Settings for Your iPad 2.")

6. To type characters that aren't on the keyboard, such as accented vowels used in many non-English languages, press and hold on the related letter or symbol. A floating menu of alternative versions for the character appears, as shown previously in Figure 3.1.

7. To delete the previously typed character, press the backspace key.

8. To end a sentence with a period, double-press the spacebar. The iPad 2 automatically inserts a period and a space instead of two spaces.

For entering numbers and punctuation, or other special characters, do the following:

1. For numbers and some special characters (0-9 - / : ; ( ) $ & @ ' "), plus the four special characters found on all keyboards (. , ? !), press the 123 key, or number key. This brings up the numbers keyboard, as shown in Figure 3.2.

FIGURE 3.2 The Numbers keyboard.

2. For special characters ([ ] { } # % ^ * + = _ | ~ < > £), plus quotes (' ") found on both special characters keyboards, plus the four special characters found on all keyboards (. , ? !), press the

#+= key, or symbol key. This brings up the symbols keyboard, as shown in Figure 3.3. (Some characters are mentioned here again because those characters are available on multiple keyboards.)

FIGURE 3.3   The Symbols keyboard in landscape mode.

Getting to the number keys and symbol keys is a hassle, as is trying to remember which special keys are on which keyboard. Practice will help, and so will little workarounds. One example is typing an ellipsis (...) instead of a dash in notes to yourself, so you don't need to switch to a different onscreen keyboard for just one character.

There are some things you can do relating to text entry beyond the standard keyboard, number keyboard, and symbol keyboard, such as the following:

▶ **Use international keyboards**—Add access to international keyboards, as described in Lesson 5. When you've enabled multiple keyboards, press and hold the Next Keyboard key to see a different keyboard. (The Next Keyboard key doesn't appear if there is only one main keyboard set up.)

▶ **Put the keyboard away**—Press the button in the lower right that looks like a keyboard to put the keyboard away. Press in a text entry area again to bring the keyboard back.

▶ **Lock the screen**—Having screen content shift orientations is confusing, but having the keyboard keep changing orientations is maddening. Use the Screen Lock switch, described in Lesson 1, "Introducing iPad 2," to prevent this.

▶ **Make a lap desk**—If you have the iPad 2 Smart Cover from
Apple (see Lesson 1), you can fold it to create an angled support
for the iPad 2 that functions like a lap desk.

Using External Keyboards

The iPad 2 has several options for using an external keyboard, as follows:

▶ Using the Apple wireless keyboard from Apple (see Lesson 1)

▶ Using a wireless Bluetooth keyboard from another provider

▶ Using an iPad 2 keyboard dock from another provider

TIP: **Get into Good Habits**

Try to develop a habitual way of entering text, using either portrait
mode or landscape mode for most or all of your typing work. Good
typing requires muscle memory, and the orientation of the screen
has a big effect on where the keys are. So, having a habitual setting
improves your ability to type quickly without thinking about it.

TIP: **Making the Keyboard Go Away**

After you establish a Bluetooth connection with an external keyboard (see Lesson 4, "Getting Connected to Wi-Fi, 3G, and
Bluetooth"), the onscreen keyboard disappears. This allows you to
see much more of the web page, document, or other area you type
into, which is a big advantage of using an onscreen keyboard.

The external keyboard gives you several advantages, as follows:

▶ Rapid entry of text, digits, and symbols.

▶ Rapid movement of the insertion point or focus point for viewing
and selection using cursor keys.

▶ Control of system functions, such as brightness, media playback,
and sound volume, on the keyboard.

If you use a keyboard not designed for use with the iPad 2, some of the keys may not be supported by the iPad 2.

CAUTION: **Getting the Keyboard Back**
If you use an external keyboard, the onscreen keyboard disappears. It may remain hidden even after you turn off the external keyboard or take it out of range. If this happens, turn off Bluetooth in the Settings app (see Lesson 4 for details). The onscreen keyboard will then reappear when needed.

External keyboards available at this writing don't provide mouse-type functionality, nor help in making selections. Many onscreen functions therefore still require you to touch the screen directly.

Inserting Text Using the Interactive Dictionary

The iPad 2 suggests completed versions and corrected versions of words you're typing. This function is called the Dictionary, but there are no word definitions in this Dictionary—only lists of words. It's just to support fast and accurate text entry.

The Dictionary automatically replaces "bad" words with "good" alternatives that it suggests. (This is called Auto-Correction, and you can turn it off in the General area of the Settings, under Keyboard, if you want.) This is marvelous when it works, which for most people seems to be most of the time. It's a tremendous pain when it doesn't work, however, and replaces your carefully chosen rare or foreign word with an incorrect alternative. (For instance, if you're caring enough to want to send "besos" in an email note—"kisses" in Spanish—the Dictionary may replace it with "besis.") Auto-Correct is automatically turned off when you're using an external keyboard.

The Dictionary also "learns." It gradually promotes suggestions that you use, and replaces suggestions you reject with the word you actually use. So, if you send "besos" enough times, the Dictionary will eventually stop changing it for you.

I recommend that you use the Dictionary as follows:

▶ **Inspect the suggestion**—Type the first few characters of a longer word—try typing three or four characters—then look at what suggestion the Dictionary has made. If it's not correct, add characters up to the end of the word, checking to see if the suggestion updates to the correct word.

▶ **Accept the suggestion**—If and when the suggestion is correct, accept the suggestion by pressing space, a punctuation mark, or the return character—just as if you had completed typing the word. The suggested word will appear onscreen.

▶ **Reject the suggestion**—If you finish typing the entire word and the suggestion is incorrect, press the suggestion before pressing space, a punctuation mark, or the return character. Pressing the suggestion dismisses it—which I, for one, find confusing. The Dictionary gradually learns to offer you the word you've typed when you start typing the same initial characters again.

To get the most out of Dictionary, I suggest that you develop an active strategy for using it. The goal is to type as little as possible, use the Dictionary as much as possible in the here and now, and train the Dictionary as much as possible for the future.

Editing with Cut, Copy, and Paste

One of the great challenges of touchscreens—indeed, a source of great inadequacy with non-touchscreen computers, too, until the mouse came along—has always been editing text. Editing requires fine control to specify the starting and stopping points for the selection, followed by quick access to options to choose the right one. Perfect for a mouse; difficult just about any other way.

The iPad 2 has perhaps the best touchscreen version of cut, copy, and paste to date, but it still takes time and practice to use correctly. Here's how to do it:

1. Double-tap a word to select it.

The word appears with three controls: two selection markers called *grab bars*, one at the beginning and one at the end of the word, and a menu of options, as shown in Figure 3.4.

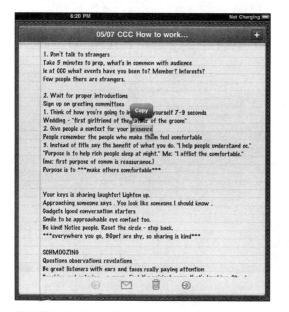

FIGURE 3.4   Mark the insertion starting and ending points.

The menu has different options depending on whether the text is editable. For editable text, such as in an email or Notes document that you're working on, the options will include Cut, Copy, and Replace, plus Paste if there is an existing selection that you can paste in. (In this case, Replace refers to replacing a word with a similar word from the Dictionary. It does not mean "Replace with text that you previously copied"; Paste does that.)

2. To act on the selection, tap one of the options from the menu.

3. To change the selection, tap the blue button on the starting grab bar or the ending grab bar.

A magnifying glass appears, as shown in Figure 3.5.

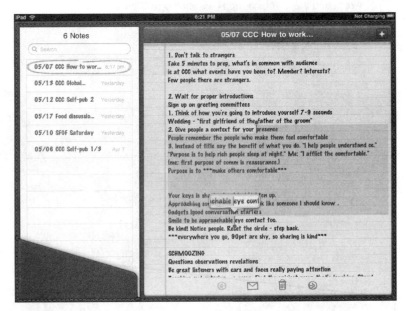

FIGURE 3.5   Use the magnifying glass to find your selection beginning or ending point.

4. While continuing to hold, drag your finger to move around the magnifying glass and, thereby, the grab bar. Look closely in the magnifying glass to see just where you've moved the grab bar to. Release to set the new beginning or ending point of the selection.

5. To cancel the selection, press anywhere in the text.

For editable text, a new insertion point appears where you tap.

Using Multi-Touch

The iPad 2 screen supports the sophisticated use of a technology called multi-touch. Multi-touch includes direct manipulation of onscreen objects by touch, as well as various special commands, called gestures, also specified by touch.

Multi-touch enables you to use gestures on the screen's surface to indicate commands to the system software or an application. A multi-touch gesture is a specific way of touching the screen to get a specific result. For instance, moving your finger rapidly across the screen—*swiping*—can move you to the next screenful of content, showing an additional pane (on the Home screen) or the next album (in the iPod app). Putting two fingers onscreen and bringing them together (pinching) zooms in when using the Maps app; the opposite gesture (spreading) zooms out.

The advantages of multi-touch include its speed, directness, and ease of use. Most multi-touch gestures seem obvious, and you may indeed find yourself using them without really thinking about it. Other times, though, you may try a gesture that seems like it should work, but doesn't. (For instance, you can't zoom in or out on text in the Notes app.) For greater ease and efficiency, it's worth taking the time to be aware of the controls available on the iPad 2, including multi-touch controls.

You should also be aware of differences in how multi-touch is implemented among apps. For instance, some apps that deal with multiple data items, such as Notes with its separate notes, don't allow swiping between them. (Swiping is defined later in this lesson.) Instead, you use arrow icons onscreen. You may have to experiment to find out which multi-touch gestures are supported by the app you're using.

Opening and Moving Among Applications

Applications on the iPad 2 are commonly referred to as *apps*, a name taken from the famous App Store that offers various Apple and third-party applications for the iPhone and iPad 2.

To open an app, start from the Home screen. Press the icon of the app you want to open the app.

To return to the Home screen, press the Home button, which will close the current app. However, some background services may continue. For instance, a song that you start in the iPod app continues playing while you switch to and use another app.

Scrolling, Swiping, and Flicking

To move directly to the top of a list or a page, tap the status bar at the top of the screen. The options are scrolling, swiping, and flicking:

▶ *Scrolling*—moving up and down in a page or list by using a control called a *scroll bar*—is a commonly used function among computer applications. On the iPad 2, using multi-touch, you scroll by dragging your finger up and down on the screen. The iPad 2 recognizes the scrolling gesture as distinct from selection, which is also done by touching the screen, but without the up-and-down dragging motion.

▶ *Swiping* is an additional multi-touch function. Swiping is done by dragging the current screen left or right. The current screen content is replaced by the page or item that is "next to" the current one among the data items managed by the app.

The choice of what is "next to" the current item is determined by the application. For instance, in the Photos app, if you have a folder of photos open, you can view one, and then move to other photos in the folder by swiping. In Maps and Safari, you move among currently open maps or web pages, respectively, by swiping.

▶ *Flicking* is a quick, repeated scrolling or swiping gesture, with less overall movement. Use flicking to move through a list or among items quickly.

To select an item, press and hold it. This might cause a word to be selected, a song to play, or detailed information about an item (such as a contact in your Contacts list) to appear.

After you select an item, a Back button (left-pointing curved arrow) may appear in the upper-left corner of the screen. Press the Back button to return to the list.

Zooming In and Out

Zooming in and out of various data items is done in two ways, as follows:

▶ **Pinching and spreading**—A pinching gesture zooms into an item, such as a map. To pinch, place two fingertips onscreen, some distance apart, and then bring them together. You will zoom into the item: a smaller area of the item will expand to fill the screen, enabling you to see greater detail.

▶ **Double-press and pressing with two fingers**—In many items, such as web pages, it can be useful to be able to quickly zoom in or out by a predetermined amount. In some apps, you can double-press (press twice quickly) onscreen to quickly zoom in by a predetermined amount. To zoom back out, you press once, with two fingers at the same time.

Summary

In this lesson, you learned how to enter text from the iPad 2 screen using the onscreen keyboard, the Dictionary, and external keyboards. You also learned how to use multi-touch on the iPad 2 screen. In the next lesson, you learn how to get and stay connected to the Internet and to external devices as much as possible, using Wi-Fi, 3G, and Bluetooth.

LESSON 4

Getting Connected to Wi-Fi, 3G, and Bluetooth

This lesson helps you learn how to get connected—and stay connected—to Wi-Fi hot spots; to 3G cell phone data coverage, if your iPad has 3G support; and to Bluetooth when (and only when) you need it.

3G or Wi-Fi?

Wi-Fi is the preferred way to connect your iPad to the Internet. It's also, usually, the only way for those of us who own an iPad 2 Wi-Fi model rather than an iPad 2 Wi-Fi+3G model.

Wi-Fi is another name for a wireless local area network, or WLAN. A WLAN works via *hot spots*, the name for a wireless router that sends out and receives radio waves that are modulated to send and receive data to the Internet.

Wi-Fi hot spots are becoming nearly ubiquitous in some people's lives. There's a high likelihood that you have Wi-Fi access both at home and at work. You may also be able to get on Wi-Fi for free at friends' homes, on school campuses, in coffee shops, in meeting places, and even on the train. There's also paid Wi-Fi access in airports, additional cafes, and covering broad areas of cities. So, Wi-Fi access may be enough for you and your iPad.

When you're in hot spot range, Wi-Fi is fast and reliable—rock solid in comparison to 3G coverage. It also uses less battery power than 3G.

There are more and more ways to get a Wi-Fi hot spot, too:

▶ **MiFi**—A MiFi is a portable wireless hot spot that basically picks up a cellular network signal and converts it into a roaming Wi-Fi hot spot. Up to five devices, such as an iPad 2, a notebook computer, and so on, can connect to the hot spot. For several months before the iPad 2 came out, Verizon sold a bundle of a MiFi unit, a Wi-Fi-only original iPad, and a data plan, showing how practical the MiFi approach is.

▶ **Portable hot spots for smartphones**—More and more smartphones support portable Wi-Fi hot spots, which is basically a MiFi built in to a smartphone. Android phones added this feature in 2010, and Apple added it to the iPhone around the time of the iPad 2 launch early in 2011 as well. This means that a very large number of potential iPad 2 buyers have a portable hot spot in their smartphone; no more need for a 3G iPad 2 model.

None of this is perfect; the MiFi is an extra device to hassle with, and running a portable hot spot from your smartphone eats battery life quickly. They're both solid options, though, especially for occasional, rather than consistent, use.

With the original iPad, more and more users found that they could do just fine with a Wi-Fi-only model. Even people with Wi-Fi+3G models found that they didn't use the 3G connection as much as they thought they would. Some rarely, if ever, even bothered to have a data plan in place to make the 3G connection available.

The same is likely to be true for the iPad 2, and even more so. First, consider all the cell phones with portable hot spots. Second, having a Wi-Fi+3G model can be a hassle for several reasons:

▶ **AT&T or Verizon?**—It's nice to have a choice of data plan providers, but the choice is not an easy one. AT&T uses GSM technology, which means it works in most other countries, which is great for travelers. Verizon's network is a bit slower, compared to AT&T's best performance, but much more reliable within the U.S. So, neither has everything a user would want.

▶ **Which data plan?**—Neither AT&T nor Verizon offers an unlimited data plan for the iPad 2 at this writing. That forces 3G iPad 2 users to guesstimate how much data transfer capacity they need per month—and pay hefty overage charges if they exceed the limit.

▶ **Why not 4G?**—Apple chose not to include 4G capability in the iPad 2, which probably made sense at the time, but more and more smartphones have 4G capability. After you get a 4G smartphone that supports tethering—portable Wi-Fi hot spot connections—you'll probably get better performance by tethering than by running off an iPad 2's built-in 3G capability.

There are cost implications as well. Apple charges $130 more, at this writing, for a 3G model than for an otherwise comparable Wi-Fi-only iPad. Plus, data coverage costs $15 a month for limited use on AT&T (up to 250MB of data transferred) and up to $80 a month for nearly unlimited use (up to 10GB of data transferred) on Verizon. You can cancel or restart the option at any point, but then, of course, you're not getting the use of the iPad 2 feature you paid extra to have available.

The two-year cost of the 3G option plus coverage, if you subscribe continuously, is anywhere from about $500 for very limited use, up to about $2,000 for nearly unlimited use, more than tripling the total cost of your iPad. And you pay more—much more—for a worse connection than you get when you can connect to a Wi-Fi network (especially if the Wi-Fi hot spot is provided by a device running off a 4G connection; zoom, zoom, zoom!). Tethering and MiFi can cost money, though. While prices vary, tethering is free for many Android phones, while one provider charges $20 a month for tethering support for the iPhone. MiFi usually costs somewhat more than that.

It's always hard to pass up options, but you should probably pass up the 3G option if you can—and, if you do get the 3G option, buy a 3G data plan only when you really need to. The rest of the time, consider finding hot spots where you can, or get a MiFi or a cell phone with portable hot spot capability.

TIP: **3G Is Good for Location Services**

Location services on a device like the iPad 2 are often referred to as "GPS capability," but GPS is only part of the story. Wireless networks and cell phone networks, if available, provide a big boost as well. If you have 3G available and turned on, your iPad 2's location services will work better. However, the functionality of the main location tool in the iPad 2, the Maps app from Google, is somewhat restricted on the iPad 2. For instance, the Maps app provides full turn-by-turn directions when running on Android-based systems, but not on iOS-based systems such as the iPad 2. So, although location services work better with 3G capability, they still won't do everything some other systems do. On iOS-based systems, turn-by-turn directions are available from some third-party apps, all of which cost money at this writing. These apps work much better with 3G, and its included hardware GPS support, than without.

Connecting via Wi-Fi

Wi-Fi is the best way to connect to the Internet, as described at the beginning of this lesson. It can be a hassle to find and log in to the nearest hot spot, but the following are a few reasons you should do so whenever possible, even if you have a 3G iPad, and a fast data connection seems to be available:

▶ **Speed**—The transfer speeds you experience via Wi-Fi vary, but are generally significantly faster than even the best and most reliable 3G connection.

▶ **Reliability**—3G connections are unreliable in many areas, a situation that's only getting worse as devices like the iPad 2 encourage increasing use of 3G data transfer. (See the 3G section later in the lesson.)

TIP: **Look for Wi-Fi Access**

Take the time to find out where Wi-Fi is available as you move about with your iPad 2, to get Wi-Fi passwords where needed, and to find out about free and paid Wi-Fi services that may be a good lifeline if you need an Internet connection (even if you have 3G capability, for the reasons stated previously). Wi-Fi access helps you get the most out of your iPad 2.

▶ **Power use**—Wi-Fi uses less power than 3G, and being connected to Wi-Fi enables you to turn off cell phone data network access, saving more power. Using a bit less electricity is good for the environment, even when you're not worried about running out of battery power.

Follow these steps to join a nearby Wi-Fi network from your iPad 2:

1. Choose Settings, Wi-Fi. Use the slider to turn on Wi-Fi.

   A list of available networks appears, as shown in Figure 4.1. A lock icon appears for networks that require a password. Some networks require you to pay for access.

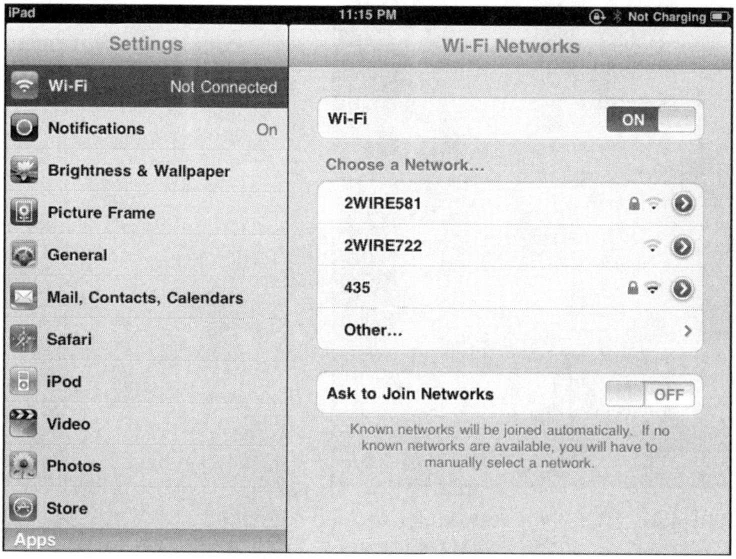

FIGURE 4.1 Log in to the best available network.

A symbol with one to three arcs filled in indicates the signal strength for each network. (You'll notice that the lowest-strength networks tend to appear and disappear from the list as the level of local interference changes and makes a network just reachable, or puts it just out of reach.)

2. Wait a moment to allow available networks to appear, and then press to select a network. If no password is required, you'll join the network immediately.

   If a password is required to join the network, a request for the password appears, as shown in Figure 4.2. Passwords are sometimes available on the wireless router itself, or from a system administrator or customer service person nearby.

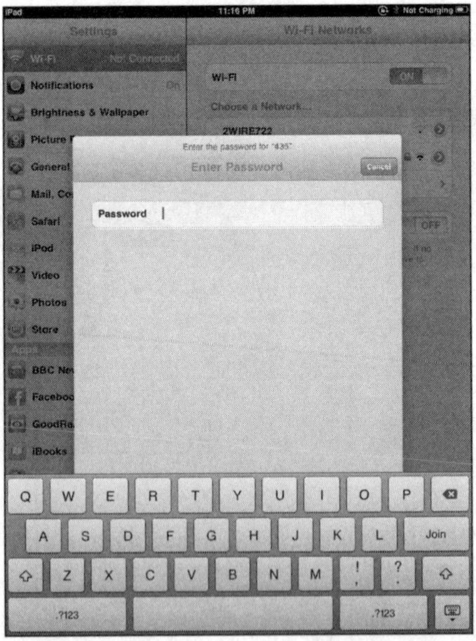

FIGURE 4.2   Enter the password for secured networks.

3. Enter the password, if required. You'll join the network. After this, your iPad 2 will remember the password, and you'll join the network immediately whenever you're in range.

4. To view technical details of the network, press the blue arrow next to the network.

   Technical details of the network appear, as shown in Figure 4.3. For systems that you've previously logged in to, an option to forget the network also appears.

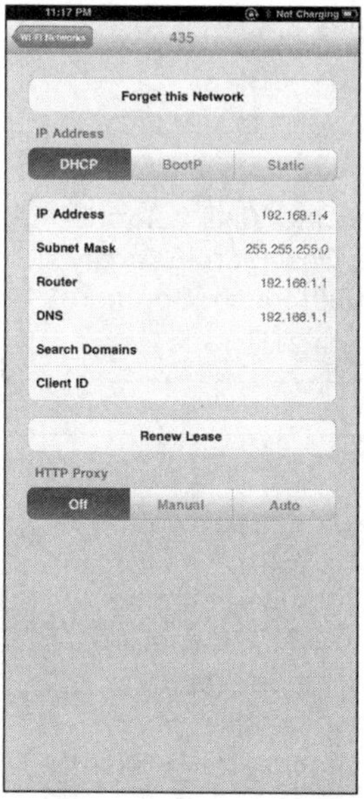

FIGURE 4.3 Ignore the technical details in most cases and just forget this network, or don't.

5. To forget a network—that is, to have your iPad 2 erase the stored password for it—press the Forget This Network button. The iPad 2 erases the stored password for this network. This prevents your iPad 2 from automatically joining this network when you are in range, allowing you to give preference to another nearby network simply by visiting that network (and not forgetting it afterward). In the future, your iPad 2 automatically joins the most recently used network out of those in range that it has previously joined.

The specific instructions for managing individual wireless networks can be summed up differently as a procedure for automatically connecting to the best available hot spot, as follows:

▶ Inspect the available networks.

▶ Decide which one you want to prefer.

▶ Join it. Your iPad 2 will then automatically keep connecting to this network first whenever the network is in range.

▶ To avoid automatically joining a network, forget it, as described in the preceding steps.

TIP: **The Status Bar Shows Your Connection**

The connection strength for the currently connected Wi-Fi network is shown in the status bar. See the "Using the Onscreen Keyboard" section of Lesson 3, "Editing Text and Using Multi-Touch," for more information about status bar icons.

NOTE: **Tether to Your Phone if You Can**

You may have a phone that supports a portable hot spot; on the iPhone, this feature is called Personal Hotspot. On Android, it's called Portable Wi-Fi Hotspot. Although each setup is a bit different, the overall process for connecting to a portable hot spot from your iPad is generally like this: Turn on your phone and go into the settings area. Turn on the hot spot feature. Then connect your iPad to the Wi-Fi network that's created, using the steps in this section. Try to connect and disconnect fairly rapidly, so you can turn off the hot spot feature on your phone; it runs the battery down fast. Bring your phone charger with you if you need to use the hot spot feature for an extended amount of time.

Connecting via 3G

The name 3G for some iPad 2 models is a bit of a misnomer. It really means that your iPad 2 can connect to the Internet using cellular data networks at speeds up to 3G. The other connection options are GPRS (2G) and, in some countries, EDGE (2.5G). So, 3G really means "cellular data networks at the fastest available speed—GPRS, EDGE, or 3G."

CAUTION: **Look Out for Some Free Networks**

Some networks have no access restrictions due to being deliberately made freely available, or accidentally being left freely available, or being set up and run for malicious purposes, such as data stealing. It's illegal to knowingly tap into a free network that doesn't expressly permit public access, and dangerous to the security of your data and iPad 2 software to risk tapping into a malicious one.

Don't join a free network unless and until you know who's offering it and that they're trustworthy.

Having 3G as the best option is understandable as of the iPad 2's introduction in the spring of 2011, but 4G networks were already beginning to be available at that time. By the time the next iPad is introduced, 4G may well be a part of it.

Any of the types of data network connection is adequate for background tasks like downloading email or broadcasting your location to social networking sites that use it for various purposes. However, interactive tasks such as web surfing and getting directions benefit greatly from the higher speed and responsiveness of EDGE or, particularly, 3G—when it works reliably.

You can expect to get a GPRS data connection just about anywhere you can get a wireless signal adequate for a phone call. EDGE and 3G connections are progressively more limited in coverage areas and are therefore unavailable in some areas.

Unfortunately for all concerned, the very usefulness and popularity of 3G means that, where there is coverage, the network is often overcrowded in certain areas. Poor implementation of all the networks means that service doesn't gracefully degrade from one level of service to the next among cell phone voice service and the data network connections—3G, EDGE, and GPRS.

Instead, every device fights for 3G bandwidth for every application, truly high-priority or not. When the 3G service gets overcrowded, cell phone calls can't be made or get dropped, web page downloads freeze, and more. Unfortunately, you can't make your 3G iPad 2 use a lesser protocol if you're having problems.

TIP: Use Wi-Fi When You Can

You use additional battery power with 3G, and in some areas 3G connections are unavailable, or slow and unreliable. Get in the habit of using Wi-Fi whenever possible, and use 3G only when you have to.

There are two requirements for 3G service on your iPad 2, as follows:

▶ A built-in 3G radio receiver, which is built in to iPad 2 Wi-Fi+3G models—and unavailable on iPad 2 Wi-Fi-only models.

▶ 3G data service, available on a month-by-month basis, as described at the beginning of this lesson. In the U.S., 3G data service is available from AT&T and Verizon, the cellular phone and data service providers for different versions of the iPhone. AT&T is infamous for its spotty 3G performance in major urban areas; Verizon's network is considered more reliable, but a Verizon-compatible iPad 2 won't work in most countries you might travel to outside the U.S.

You may want to check 3G coverage in the areas where you live, work, and frequently visit to find out what the promised level of 3G coverage is, and then talk to people in the affected areas to learn about the level of support you can actually expect.

When traveling outside of your provider's service area, you may be able to get data roaming support—but if you just log on and start using it on arrival, it's likely to be very, very expensive. Check with your home provider before traveling, and see if you can get a reasonably priced roaming plan before you leave your usual service area.

CAUTION: **Turn Off Data Roaming**

To avoid data roaming charges, make sure the Data Roaming setting is turned off, as described here. If you do turn on the Data Roaming setting to use roaming services for some period of time, be sure to turn it off immediately afterward.

Follow these steps to manage the use of cellular data networking service on your iPad 2 Wi-Fi+3G:

1. To set up or stop a cellular data plan, tap the Settings icon, and choose Cellular Data and then Cellular Data Plan. Follow the onscreen instructions. (You will need to obtain a micro-SIM card before using cellular data.) Visit the same Settings area if and when you want to stop your plan.

2. To turn off data roaming, tap the Settings icon and choose Cellular Data. If data roaming is On, turn the slider to Off.

3. Turn off all iPad 2 radio transmitters—Wi-Fi, cellular data, GPS, and Bluetooth—by tapping Airplane Mode in Settings (Airplane mode is available only on iPad 2 Wi-Fi+3G, not on Wi-Fi-only models). On some airplanes, you may then be allowed to turn on Wi-Fi, not 3G, to use onboard Wi-Fi services, possibly at an extra charge.

Using Bluetooth

Bluetooth is very different from Wi-Fi, as it's normally used to connect to nearby devices, not to the Internet. Bluetooth is a very limited-range communications protocol that's used to link your iPad 2 to a device, such as a keyboard, without the need for wires. However, you do need to turn off Bluetooth when you're not using it, both to save power and to close a potential open door for hackers who want your device's data and connections.

Bluetooth—described at the beginning of this lesson—is used for peripheral devices, such as a wireless keyboard or wireless headphones, at distances of up to a few feet.

To use your iPad 2's Bluetooth connection with a specific device, you have to pair them.

Follow these steps to pair a Bluetooth device with the iPad 2:

1. Look at the instructions for the device in question and take the steps needed to make it discoverable.

   These steps are usually fairly simple. On the Apple Bluetooth keyboard, for instance, you simply turn on the keyboard. Other devices may require some combination of button presses. Check the printed or online documentation for the device.

2. In the Settings application, tap General, and then Bluetooth, and slide the Bluetooth option to On.

   The iPad 2 will display a list of devices it has successfully paired with and start searching for new, discoverable Bluetooth devices.

3. The iPad 2 will discover the nearby device and ask you to con-
firm that it is the appropriate one by entering some kind of code.

For instance, for the Apple Bluetooth keyboard, the iPad 2 will
ask you to enter a PIN by typing on the numeric keys of the
device, as shown in Figure 4.4.

FIGURE 4.4   The iPad 2 asks for help in pairing.

4. Quickly complete the requested step.

If you don't complete the step in time, the process will time out,
and you'll have to restart.

5. If you complete the step requested on time, the device will pair
with the iPad 2. If you fail to complete the step requested on
time, turn off Bluetooth and then start over.

When the pairing is successful, you will not have to complete the
pairing process again in normal use, although the device may
"forget" that it is paired if it loses power. In this case, repeat the
pairing process.

6. After you have paired a device, if you stop using it, you should
clear it from the iPad 2's memory. To do this, choose the device
from the list on the Bluetooth screen. On the screen that appears,
choose Forget this Device.

The device will be unpaired. If you want to re-pair it, you may need to
remove the power connection and/or batteries from the device so that it
forgets it was previously paired and gives you the opportunity to re-pair it.

> CAUTION: **Keep Bluetooth Off**
>
> Bluetooth connections are a potential target of hackers who can move through public places, looking for data they can steal over Bluetooth. Bluetooth also uses additional battery power. Be sure to turn off Bluetooth whenever you're not using it.

Summary

In this lesson, you learned how to connect to the Internet using Wi-Fi and, if available on your iPad 2 model, 3G. You also learned how to pair Bluetooth devices to your iPad 2. In the next lesson, you will learn how to customize settings for your iPad 2.

LESSON 5

Customizing General Settings for Your iPad 2

This lesson explains how to use the iPad 2's General Settings to manage the overall system, including storage, international and language settings, restrictions, additional keyboards, and more.

Managing iPad 2 Settings

Settings often hold many secrets to getting a device to work well and to fit the way you use it. The iPad 2's settings, however, are somewhat different from the settings on other computing devices, with much less under the control of the user than on other systems. With the iPad 2, you are unable to set the system font or the size of displayed characters. Neither data files nor program files are directly accessible on the device at all.

As a longtime computer user, right back to Apple II days, I found the locked-down nature of the iPad and iPad 2 frustrating at first. However, I often find myself picking up my iPad 2 to get things done while my Windows PC is rebooting, installing software, or some other time-consuming task. That's just one proof point for the advantages of the iPad 2's simpler approach.

The iPad 2 does have some helpful features among its settings, though. These include very flexible use of onscreen and external keyboards for a variety of languages and character sets, as well as strong accessibility options.

It's still valuable to review the available settings on the iPad 2 to see what you can do, but equally to see what you can't do. That way, you won't waste time looking for a setting that isn't there.

Table 5.1 summarizes the available options. Learn what is available, and then enjoy getting the most out of your iPad 2 as you use it.

TABLE 5.1 General Settings Described in Detail in This Lesson

Category	Functionality
About	Lists the number of items from different media types on your iPad 2 and shows available capacity and technical details.
Sounds	Turns sound on and off for mail received and sent, calendar, lock, and keyboard.
Auto-Lock	Option to turn on the screen saver and require a button slide to allow access after a delay that you specify.
Passcode Lock	Option to lock iPad 2 and require a four-digit code to allow access after a delay that you specify.
Restrictions	Option to restrict access to many built-in iPad 2 apps and to mature content for music, movies, TV shows, and apps.
Side Switch	Controls whether the side switch is used as a screen orientation lock or a mute switch.
Date & Time	Sets time format, time zone, and system date and time.
Keyboard	Sets keyboard interactivity options; adds onscreen and external keyboards in various formats.
International	Sets language; sets region format for system display of dates, times, and phone numbers.
Battery %	Option to display specific percentage of battery life remaining.
Reset	Option to reset all settings; to erase all settings; or to reset settings specifically for networking, the keyboard dictionary, the Home screen layout, or location warnings.

> NOTE: **Take Your Time with Settings**
>
> This lesson summarizes only some of the settings and their effects. Take the time to look through and experiment with settings to understand them and what each one does in more detail. Doing so can help you get the most out of your iPad 2.

About

The About area (see Figure 5.1) displays specifics that help you manage storage on your device, along with some other not-so-important details.

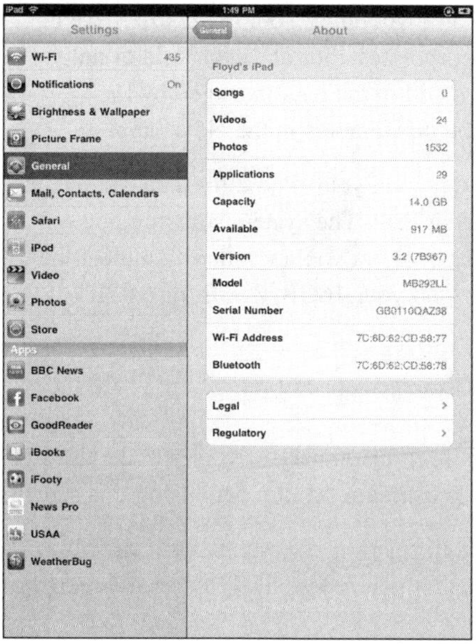

FIGURE 5.1 Your iPad offers you a storage overview and system specifics.

The important areas for managing storage are as follows:

▶ **Songs**—Songs in MP3 format take up about 1MB per minute of time in the song. A typical three-minute pop song takes up about 3MB.

▶ **Videos**—Videos can be short clips or long movies, highly compressed or HD-quality. Higher-quality videos take up about 10MB per 1 minute of time in the video. That means a 100-minute, high-quality movie takes up about 1GB—a big chunk of the total space available on any iPad 2, especially the 16GB models.

▶ **Photos**—Photos can be high-resolution monsters of 5MB or even unprocessed image files that take up 15MB each. They can also be small, compressed versions that just take up 100KB or so. At 1MB each—a typical size if you're a bit careful with your settings—you can fit about 14,000 photos on a 16GB iPad 2.

▶ **Applications**—Apps vary widely (and wildly). An app can be almost unnoticeably small or a whopping 100MB in size—even larger if, for instance, it incorporates a lot of video. Additionally, an app size increases as you add to the data managed by the app—for instance, when you create notes in the Notes app.

▶ **Capacity**—This is the "budget" on your iPad 2 for data—songs, videos, photos, apps, and their data. The system software and data takes up approximately 2GB, so you are left with almost the full use of the flash memory on your 16GB, 32GB, or 64GB iPad 2.

▶ **Available**—The amount of storage capacity remaining.

Unfortunately, the iPad 2 doesn't offer a summary of your storage use by type of data. Your only choice is to estimate the numbers using this screen.

In addition to the storage-related information, the About area has some potentially important information that you're less likely to need directly, as follows:

▶ **Version; Model; Serial Number; Wi-Fi Address; Bluetooth.** Specific technical information that you may need to look up for technical support or other purposes.

▶ **Legal; Regulatory.** Apple is required to make certain information available on the machine. This is where you'll find it.

Sounds

Sounds enables you to set an overall range for system-level sounds—from completely muted to full volume—and to set which system events trigger sounds. The choices are as follows:

▶ **Ringtone**—The sound you hear when you receive a call on FaceTime.

▶ **New Mail and Sent Mail**—Get alerted as emails come in and go out.

▶ **Calendar Alerts**—Help calendar items get your attention.

▶ **Lock Sounds**—When you lock the screen orientation on your iPad 2, for instance, you can hear a satisfying click.

▶ **Keyboard Clicks**—This gives you audio feedback as to whether you touched no keys, one, or more than one.

Each option has its own preset sounds. To hear the different sounds, use the slider to turn an option off, then on. As you turn on the option, you'll hear its assigned sound. Then you are able to choose whether to turn that sound on or off.

Network

Network has two sets of settings: VPN, or a Virtual Private Network, and Wi-Fi.

A Virtual Private Network gives users the feeling of being directly connected to a company or other organization's network while using the publicly available Internet as "plumbing" for carrying data and control information. This requires a lot of technical settings that you won't normally need to be concerned with.

The organization that supplies your VPN should also supply setup information. Or, your organization may physically take your iPad 2 from you, set it up on your VPN, test that everything works, and return it to you, along with instructions on how to use it effectively and securely.

The second set of settings is for Wi-Fi. Wi-Fi settings are more commonly accessed through the Wi-Fi Settings option at the top of the Settings list, which presents exactly the same screens and options as if you come into the Wi-Fi settings via the Network option. Wi-Fi settings are discussed in the previous lesson.

Bluetooth

Bluetooth settings help you attach, or "pair," Bluetooth devices to your iPad 2, and manage security and power usage by turning off Bluetooth when not in active use. Bluetooth settings are described in the previous lesson under the heading, "Using Bluetooth."

Location Services

Location Services includes the GPS radio in your iPad 2 and the software that supports it. See Lesson 11, "Working with Maps," for more on GPS and how it works in conjunction with Wi-Fi and, if available, 3G on your iPad 2.

CAUTION: **Turn Off GPS When You Can**

The GPS radio in the iPad 2 3G uses a considerable amount of power, so turn it off when possible. You'll want to have it on, though, when using the Maps app or geo-aware apps and websites.

An app or website will not necessarily tell you to turn on your system's GPS radio to provide information—it will provide geo-aware services if information location is available and won't provide them (or not provide them very well) if it isn't. Therefore, it's up to you to figure out when you need Location Services turned on (for more functionality) or off (to save power).

Auto-Lock

Auto-Lock is the function that controls the frequency of the unlocking operation you go through when you use your iPad 2. There isn't a security aspect to this; it just turns off the screen, saving power and providing privacy for you with regard to the screen's contents. Auto-Lock also prevents you from accidentally entering commands or characters into the iPad 2 when you're not intending to use it. (For instance, if your iPad 2 gets jostled in your bag when you're carrying it.)

> CAUTION: **Save Your Screen!**
>
> If you allow the same image to remain on your iPad 2 screen for long periods of time, a "ghost" of the image might become permanently etched into your screen's phosphors, interfering with your use and enjoyment of your iPad 2. Use Auto-Lock to turn off the screen automatically after a few minutes of non-use.

The Auto-Lock option has several possible settings: 2 minutes, 5 minutes, 10 minutes, 15 minutes, and Never. Choose the one that makes the most sense for you. In most cases, you should avoid the Never option, as it can too easily lead to wasting power and to screen burn-in.

Passcode Lock

The iPad 2 Passcode Lock setting is similar to a feature found on some personal computers and mobile phones. After a period of non-use, the system becomes blocked, and a password is required to access it again.

Passcodes make a great deal of sense for personal computers, which are likely to contain financial and other highly confidential information for yourself and/or your company. An iPad 2, however, can be used in different ways.

Your iPad 2 may have just as much confidential information, access to your email, and so on as a personal computer. In this case, using a passcode makes sense. However, if your only intent is to load your iPad 2 with things like television episodes or music, the security implications of someone accessing it without your permission may not be truly dire.

In addition, many people find passcodes (and even Auto-Lock, described in the previous section) to be a tremendous hassle and annoyance; others find them normal and reassuring. Consider your own security needs and comfort level before deciding whether and how to use Passcode Lock.

The Passcode Lock setting has several options, as follows:

> ▶ **Turn Passcode On/Off**—This option turns the entire Passcode feature off or on. See Figure 5.2 for the entry box iPad 2 uses to enable you to enter a passcode.

FIGURE 5.2   You can use passcodes for your system and for app restrictions.

▶ **Change Passcode**—Use this option to change the actual passcode you enter. Be very careful to create a passcode you will remember, as you will have a great deal of trouble getting access to your iPad 2 if it's locked and you don't have the passcode.

▶ **Require Passcode**—With this option, you can specify the amount of time that your system is unused before passcode protection goes into effect. The available options are Immediately, After 1 minute, After 5 minutes, After 15 minutes, After 1 hour, and After 4 hours.

CAUTION: **Use a Memorable Passcode**

Be sure you can remember your iPad 2 passcode, as well as any passcode you create for restrictions (described below) after you set it up or change it.

▶ **Picture Frame**—This feature enables you to view stored photos on your machine while it's locked. It can be turned on or off.

▶ **Erase Data**—Choosing this option specifies that all data on your iPad 2 will be erased after 10 failed passcode attempts. Use caution before choosing this option, because the results of your data being erased are permanent.

CAUTION: **Look Out for Dodgy Photos**

Think twice about all the photos stored on your machine before turning on Picture Frame. Some photos may be embarrassing; some may be inappropriate if displayed in a business environment, and can even be grounds for disciplinary action or termination.

Restrictions

Restrictions settings enable you to control purchasing ability for apps and websites, as well as content restrictions for media, including music, movies, TV shows, and even apps.

To enable Restrictions, press the Enable Restrictions button; the screen will then display possible restrictions, as shown in Figure 5.3. You'll be asked to enter a four-digit passcode for restrictions. As with Passcode Lock, be very careful not to set a passcode you might forget; it could cause you significant expense and hassle to override it.

Some of the built-in apps are potentially troublesome because they can be used to access content not suitable for children. You can turn off several potentially troublesome apps entirely: Safari, YouTube, iTunes, the App Store (and the ability to install apps), and Location services. After the app is disabled, its icon is removed from the Home screen.

You also have the ability to specify what content you would like to allow. The following is a list of settings relating to content that you can change:

▶ **In-App Purchases**—A growing number of apps enable you to purchase upgraded functionality, additional episodes, and even additional items or character abilities in a game, all from within the app.

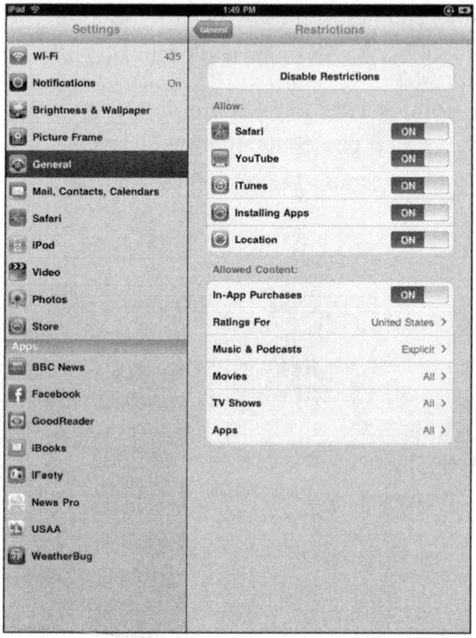

FIGURE 5.3   You can enter a range of restrictions for your iPad 2.

▶ **Ratings For**—This setting enables you to specify the country whose TV and movie ratings you want to use—Australia, Canada, France, Germany, Ireland, Japan, New Zealand, United Kingdom, or United States. Not all content will be rated in all jurisdictions.

▶ **Music & Podcasts**—You have the capability to allow or disallow content labeled Explicit.

▶ **Movies**—You may specify which level of movies to allow. For U.S. ratings, the levels are Don't Allow Movies, G, PG, PG-13, R, NC-17, or Allow All Movies.

▶ **TV Shows**—With this Restriction setting, you can specify which level of TV shows to allow. For U.S. ratings, the levels are as follows: Don't Allow TV Show, TV-Y, TV-Y7, TV-G, TV-PG, TV-14, TV-MA, or Allow All TV Shows.

▶ **Apps**—Adjusting this setting enables you to specify which level of apps to allow. The levels are the following: Don't Allow Apps, 4+, 9+, 12+, 17+, or Allow All Apps.

NOTE: **Watch Out for Racy Websites**
At this writing, apps are tightly restricted by Apple, so very little that might be considered obscene or offensive is allowed in apps. At the same time, a site such as Safari, being an unrestricted web browser, can allow you access to content that's obscene or offensive by almost anyone's definition. Websites are also poorly labeled and regulated. Unfortunately, the types of restrictions available for apps, movies, and TV shows are not available for websites. You can only make the whole web available, via Safari, or not.

Date & Time

With this function, you can turn on 24-hour (military) time, so your time appears as 2311 instead of 11:11pm. You also have the capability to set the time zone to your home city, which you may want to change when you are traveling outside of your usual time zone. If desired, you can also set the date and time directly.

Keyboard

The goal of the iPad 2's typing system is to enable you to type quickly, and even a bit carelessly, and still get good results. However, the adjustments that the iPad 2 makes for you can be a bit annoying sometimes—and, if you like to take full control of getting the details right, even downright frustrating.

If you frequently use an external keyboard and find that you're more accurate with it than with the onscreen keyboard, you may want what you type to not be changed for you by the system software. That's because you're making fewer errors, so the adjustments the iPad 2 makes are that much more likely to be causing, rather than fixing, errors.

Keyboard settings enable you to take back as much or as little control as you want to, as follows:

- ▶ **Auto-Correction**—This option controls whether entries are auto-corrected using the Dictionary. The Dictionary can be quite useful, but if you use a lot of unusual or specialist terms, or even custom abbreviations that tend to get auto-corrected into unintelligibility, you may want to turn off Auto-Correction.

- ▶ **Auto-Capitalization**—Use this option to control whether the first letter after a full stop is automatically capitalized.

- ▶ **Enable Caps Lock**—As on a physical keyboard, it's easy to accidentally enable Caps Lock on the iPad 2's onscreen keyboard. To avoid this problem, the default setting for Caps Lock is Off.

- ▶ **"." Shortcut**—This shortcut automatically converts a double-space (pressing the spacebar twice) to a period followed by a space. In combination with auto-capitalization, this creates a very easy way to end one sentence and start another, because the period at the end of one sentence and the capital letter at the beginning of another are automatically created for you simply by double-spacing.

You can also specify many options for the onscreen keyboard and any external keyboard you want to use, as follows:

- ▶ **English keyboard**—Specify whether the default English-language onscreen keyboard uses a classic QWERTY layout or a modified AZERTY or QWERTZ layout. (You might give these a try if you're not familiar with them to see if they would work better for you; plan to practice for a while before you reach full speed with the new setup.)

- ▶ **Hardware keyboard layout**—You can use many kinds of external keyboards via Bluetooth. The layouts supported are U.S., Dvorak, U.S. International—PC, U.S. Extended, British, French, German, Spanish—ISO, Italian, Dutch, and Belgian.

You can also add additional onscreen keyboards to your iPad 2, as follows:

▶ **Add New Keyboard**—This button offers choices of Chinese (Simplified) Handwriting, Chinese (Simplified) Pinyin, Dutch, English (UK), Flemish, French, French (Canada), German, Italian, Japanese, Russian, and Spanish. You can add as many keyboards as you like.

▶ **Removing an onscreen keyboard**—Bring the list of keyboards onscreen in the Keyboard Settings area, and then press Edit. A red Delete button will appear next to each keyboard. Press the Delete button for the keyboard you want to delete. If you chose to delete the English keyboard, the first keyboard listed will then become your default keyboard.

To access the additional onscreen keyboard(s) you have added, press the World key (globe icon) on your default keyboard. You can then switch between keyboards as needed.

> TIP: **iPad Keyboards Are Easy**
> Adding and using additional keyboards on iPad 2 is easy. If you need to use ideographic characters, as with Chinese or Japanese, or to flexibly mix languages, the iPad 2 may be the best option you can find.

International

Choose the appropriate internationally compliant settings for your iPad 2, as follows:

▶ **Language**—Choose among Chinese, Dutch, English, French, German, Italian, Japanese, Russian, and Spanish.

▶ **Keyboards**—Choose keyboards and add external and onscreen keyboards, as described in the previous section.

▶ **Region format**—Set the region format for date, time, and phone number layout. For instance, for the UK, the formats for date, time, and phone number would appear as follows: Tuesday, 5 January 2010; 00:34; 07700 900202.

> NOTE: **Use Country-Specific Formats**
> The iPad 2 supports dozens of regional formats for dates, times, and phone numbers, including country-specific formats for Spanish-speaking and German-speaking countries, among others.

Accessibility

The iPad 2 has a very strong set of accessibility options, which may be among the best options out there for addressing your needs for input and computing flexibility.

Battery Percentage

You have the option to display or to hide the battery percentage in the status bar. Move the slider to see the effect: You are only hiding or displaying the numeric display, such as: 98%. The icon, which displays the approximate battery charge status and whether the device is plugged in, will remain.

Reset and Profile

You can reset several groups of settings on your iPad 2 to what they were when you first purchased your iPad 2, as follows:

- ▶ **Reset All Settings**—Choose this option to clear all preferences and settings you have entered. Unlike the next option, the Reset All Settings option does not erase app data such as Contacts and Calendar entries. Media files, such as videos and songs, are also left intact.

- ▶ **Erase All Content and Settings**—Choose this option to clear all preferences and settings you have entered. Unlike the previous option, this option erases app data, such as Contacts and Calendar entries, and media such as videos and songs. (Some of this information may be recovered if and when you synch with an external source for Contacts and Calendar data, or with iTunes for media.)

► **Reset Network Settings**—Choose this option to make iPad 2
"forget" any previously used network and VPN settings, except
those installed by a configuration profile. When you choose this
option, Wi-Fi is turned off and then back on to disconnect you
from any currently connected Wi-Fi network. Wi-Fi is left on,
and the Ask to Join Networks setting is left on.

► **Reset Keyboard Dictionary**—As you use your iPad 2, the
Dictionary adds a word whenever you reject a Dictionary suggestion and use another word instead. It then stops making the suggestion it had made before. Choose this option to reset the
Dictionary, erasing all previously added words.

► **Reset Home Screen Layout**—Choose this option to return the
Home screen layout to its original settings.

► **Reset Location Warnings**—Choose this option to erase any
record of previously accepting requests for an app, such as Maps,
to use the iPad 2's Location Services, as shown in Figure 5.4.

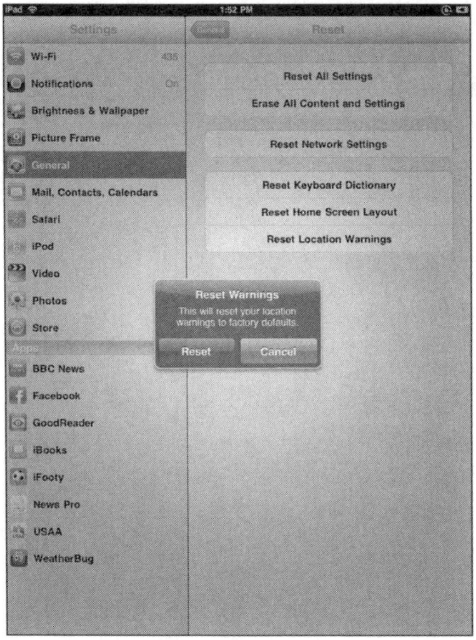

FIGURE 5.4   You can start from scratch with your iPad 2's data.

The Profiles list includes configuration profiles for VPN settings. To delete a profile, select it from the list under Profiles; then press Remove.

Summary

In this lesson, you learned how to use the iPad 2's General Settings to manage settings relating to the overall system, such as storage, international and language settings, content restrictions, and additional keyboards. In the next lesson, I'll describe using the Web on your iPad 2.

LESSON 6

Using the Web on Safari

This lesson shows you how to surf the Web from the iPad 2 using Apple's Safari browser, including viewing web pages, searching the Web, using bookmarks and web clips, and working around possible concerns with screen size and lack of Adobe Flash support. Surfing the Web requires an Internet connection; for information on getting connected, see Lesson 4, "Getting Connected to Wi-Fi, 3G, and Bluetooth."

Introducing Safari on iPad 2

Surfing the Web from the iPad 2 using Apple's Safari browser is a highlight of using the device. For some people, it's *the* highlight. Because you hold the iPad 2 in your hands and touch the screen directly, you interact with the Web differently than on a personal computer. Because the iPad 2's screen is so large compared to the screen on a cellphone, the iPad 2 experience is much better than that as well.

> NOTE: **Fitting Sites on the iPad 2 Screen**
> The iPad 2 screen is slightly smaller than most computer screens in use today; its resolution is 1024×768 pixels, whereas most laptop screens today are 1280×800. Therefore, some websites that are designed to take advantage of big screens will not quite fit onscreen on the iPad 2. Also, the iPad 2 does not support Flash, a popular format for multimedia, which means some Web multimedia won't work on your iPad 2. Many of the leading sites that use Flash—including Hulu, YouTube, and Netflix—either have an iPad app, have adapted their sites to serve non-Flash video to incoming iOS devices, or both. But restaurant and hotel sites often use Flash, and many such sites have at least some missing video clips or other functionality on the iPad 2.

Compared to the original iPad, the iPad 2 has improvements specifically designed to speed web surfing. It has a faster processor, the dual-core A5, replacing the single-core A4 chip that powers the original iPad. The iPad 2 also has a much faster graphics processor that, according to Apple, runs up to nine times faster on some graphics tests.

The increase in RAM found on the iPad 2, moving up from 256MB on the original iPad to 512MB on the iPad 2, is also a boost for graphics performance, which is RAM hungry. With improved graphics performance, web pages appear onscreen faster. Web surfing on the iPad 2 is particularly (and impressively) flexible if you have an iPad 2 Wi-Fi+3G model, rather than an iPad 2 Wi-Fi only model. (See Lesson 4 for details.)

Apple also introduced the Apple Nitro JavaScript engine along with the iPad 2. JavaScript is a key component of most modern web pages, and it's also used to help replace Flash, which the iPad 2 and other iOS devices don't support. By creating this new JavaScript engine, which is said to cut JavaScript processing times in half, Apple helps speed up web page performance and gives non-Flash web pages a further advantage over those that use Flash. The iPad 2's 1024×768 screen resolution is generous compared to smartphone screen sizes, including the iPhone's 480×320, but it's still a bit small for some web page layouts. That means that you have to scroll sideways to see parts of some web pages, which is a pain.

Also, the iPad 2 does not support Adobe Flash, which is used on many sites to control multimedia, such as video playback. This is a deliberate decision by Apple, which describes Flash as slow and prone to make computer systems crash. Flash support is unlikely to be added to the iPad family, iPhones, or the iPod Touch lineup in the future. As a result, many web page authors are rewriting their sites to avoid the use of Flash, or to serve a page that doesn't depend on Flash when an iPad or other iOS device is being used. YouTube is the most prominent example of a site that was rewritten to better support iOS devices.

The iPad's lack of Flash support means that many cool multimedia features—and even the core functionality of some entire websites—don't work at all on iPad 2. Despite these hassles, though, the iPad 2 is a great web surfing machine.

NOTE: **Alternatives to Safari**

Many browsers are available for personal computers, and many exist now for the iPad family as well. One feature that some alternative browsers have, which is lacking in Safari at this writing, is tabs within a browser window. The alternative browser that I use, Atomic Web, does a good job of making it easy to use tabs on the iPad 2.

Using Portrait and Landscape Modes

A preferred way to surf the Web with the iPad 2 is to use it in portrait mode (like the way you would usually write on a letter-size or legal-size tablet of paper). Since web pages are most often designed and used in this kind of orientation, they look great rendered that way in a device you can easily hold in your hands. Many pages work well this way, too.

One of the greatest things about using the iPad 2, though, is its always upright functionality—the page continuously rotates to follow the way that you're holding the device. There's no "wrong" way to hold an iPad 2. As with web pages, some content works better one way or the other.

This always upright functionality goes from being optional to becoming a necessity when using Safari and viewing web pages. The reason is simple: Many websites today are designed for widescreens—for instance, to fill, or almost fill, the 1280×800 resolution common on laptops. When you visit a widescreen-oriented website with the iPad 2 in portrait mode, the horizontal resolution is only 768 pixels, instead of, perhaps, 1280 pixels—a reduction of nearly half. Because of this, the page may not render very well at all. It may reflow into the much narrower space in a clumsy way, or you may need to zoom in to enlarge text on the page and make it readable.

At this writing, the InformIT site that publicizes Sams titles like the one you hold in your hand is one of these widescreen-oriented sites when viewed on a personal computer monitor. The site has a wide central column that would, by itself, come close to filling the width of an old-fashioned

800×600-resolution personal computer monitor. It has additional columns to the left and right, each about half as large as the central column.

If you look at the InformIT site using a web browser on a personal computer and then narrow the window on a personal computer to about 800 pixels, not much changes—you just lose the right-hand column until you scroll sideways.

When viewed on the iPad 2 in portrait mode, though, the site fits right in, as shown in Figure 6.1. It does this, though, by shrinking the text—perhaps to a level that's unreadable, or at least that isn't much fun to read.

FIGURE 6.1   Some screens shrink in the iPad 2's portrait mode.

Turn the iPad 2 on its side, and suddenly the text gets bigger, as shown in Figure 6.2. You don't get much content, but what you do see is quite readable. You might even find yourself using portrait mode to navigate around the site and switching to landscape mode for the parts you really want to read.

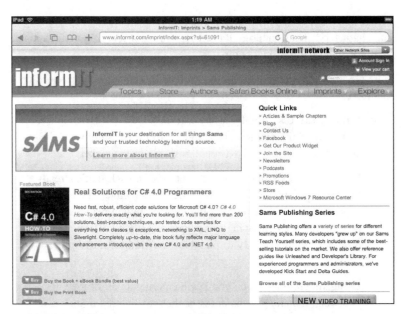

FIGURE 6.2   Web page text can be more readable in landscape mode.

TIP: **Consider Using the Same Browser**

Consider using the same browser on your personal computer (or, if you have more than one, on all your personal computers) as well as on iPad 2, so you have a consistent experience on different systems. The native iPad 2 browser, Safari, is also the native browser on the Macintosh and the iPhone and is available as a free download for Windows machines. There are several alternatives for both iPhone and iPad; check the App Store, as described in Lesson 12, for the latest and greatest.

Opening Web Pages

Opening a web page can be more difficult on an iPad 2 than on a personal computer because web URLs are a mix of letters and special characters. On a personal computer keyboard, all these keys are available at once; however, the iPad 2's onscreen keyboard spreads the same character set across three sets of keys (the alphabetical keys, the numeric keys, and special characters). Thus, entering these URLs on your iPad 2 can take longer than it would on a personal computer.

Here are a few pointers for entering a web address that can help speed up the process:

▶ **Finding the URL field**—Many websites cause the URL field to be hidden while you look at a page. Scroll up or simply tap the status bar to bring the URL field onscreen even quicker.

▶ **Deleting the existing URL**—To get rid of a URL that's already in the address bar, tap the address field and then tap the X that appears. Get in the habit of doing this before you begin entering text, because it's annoying to struggle to enter a URL via the onscreen keyboard, only to find there's a jumbled mess in the URL field.

▶ **Using shortcuts**—When you begin entering a part of the URL you want, matching web addresses that you entered in the past will appear beneath the URL you're entering. Watch the list as you type and pick out the appropriate URL as soon as it appears.

▶ **Reducing text entry**—Consider going to the home page of the site you want—even if it's not the exact URL—and then navigating within the site to reach your desired web page, instead of typing the full URL.

TIP: **How Not to Open a New Page**
Some web links, such as search results, automatically open in a new page, closing the search results page. To override this behavior, press and hold the link, and then choose Open instead of Open in New Page.

▶ **Storing web pages**—You can open multiple pages by pressing the multipage button at the top of the Safari browser. A list of currently open web pages appears (up to nine can be open at once), as shown in Figure 6.3. Tap New Page to save the previous web page for later reuse.

FIGURE 6.3   Manage stored web pages for flexibility.

▶ **Searching the Web**—Press in the search area in the upper-right corner, enter the word or phrase you want, and then tap Search. When the search results appear, press the area to open the result in a new window, or press and hold to get the option to open the result in the same window, replacing the search results.

▶ **Revisiting web pages**—Press the multipage button; then choose the previously visited web page you want from among the stored web pages. The effect of this is a lot like having nine web browser windows open at once.

> TIP: **Use History to Return to a Page**
>
> You can use History, described later in the lesson, to quickly revisit recently opened web pages. Use the multipage function more

strategically to hold sites that you may want to revisit multiple times over a longer session of using the iPad 2.

▶ **Closing unneeded web pages**—Treat the multipage function as nine "slots" that you keep filled with web pages you want to revisit. To get rid of a stored web page, open the multipage view, then press the X on the upper-left corner of the icon representing the page you want to close.

Zooming and Scrolling

The iPad 2 screen is much larger than a smartphone screen. For instance, the iPad 2 screen is about five times the size, in pixels, of an iPhone screen. It's about three-fourths the size of a typical wide-screen laptop, though, so you'll have to zoom and scroll sometimes to access content and to read text clearly.

To zoom and scroll in Safari, use the following gestures:

▶ **Zoom in or out by pinching**—Pinch or spread your fingers to move in and out of a web page.

▶ **Zoom in or out by pressing**—Double-press within a column on a web page to expand it (zoom in). Double-press again on an expanded column to compress it (zoom out).

▶ **Scroll a web page**—Press and drag up and down or sideways. The iPad 2 detects that you're scrolling and doesn't follow any links that may be under your finger.

▶ **Scroll within a frame**—Press and drag with two fingers, not just one, up and down or sideways.

▶ **Go to the top**—Press the status bar.

Navigating Web Pages

Careful navigating among web pages is particularly important on the iPad 2 because the screen space and multitasking capability are both limited.

The following tips for navigating web pages thoroughly help you get the most out of the iPad 2 and Safari:

> ▶ **Options for opening links**—You can see linking options by pressing and holding the link, as shown in Figure 6.4. A box with the destination URL (in very small type) and options will appear. Options may include Open, Open in New Page, Save Image (saves an image in the Photo Library), and Copy.

FIGURE 6.4   Open up your options by pressing and holding a link.

> ▶ **Stop loading the web page**—Press X in the address field.

> ▶ **Reload the page**—Press the round reload arrow in the address field.

> ▶ **Move to the next or previous web page**—Press the left or right arrow in the address bar, if available.

> ▶ **Access current URL options**—Press the Bookmark button in the address field, causing options to appear, as shown in Figure

FIGURE 6.5   Create web clips with Add to Home Screen, and more.

6.5. From among the options that appear, choose Add Bookmark to bookmark a page; Add to Home Screen to save a "live" icon called a web clip to the Home screen; or Mail Link to This Page to open the Mail app with an email containing the current URL. You can edit the name of a web clip before you save it.

▶ **Return to Safari**—Some links open another application, such as a Mailto link—a link to an email address—opening up the Email app, or a Maps link opening the Maps app. To return to your web page and Safari, you have to press the Home button and then press the Safari icon.

CAUTION: **Consider Surfing Differently on iPad 2**

Using slow-loading web pages on an iPad 2 can be much more frustrating than on a personal computer because it's not easy to start doing another task while you are waiting. Also, using the Web might be more fun and satisfying on the iPad 2 than on a personal computer because you interact with the web page directly on the iPad 2, but waiting for a web page to load may be more frustrating. You may find that you develop different web-surfing habits on your iPad 2 than on your personal computer—partly because of the lack of Flash support, but also because of time constraints.

Using Bookmarks

Bookmarks are great time-savers on personal computers. They're even more important on iPad 2 because of the difficulty of entering URLs as text, and also because of the limitations on screen size, making it harder to juggle multiple windows.

Follow these instructions to use bookmarks in Safari:

1. To bookmark a web page, with a web page open, press the Bookmark icon. Choose Add Bookmark. Edit the bookmark name, if desired, and use the drop-down list to place the book-mark in a folder.

   The default location for a bookmark is the Bookmarks Bar, which is a drop-down menu from the top bar of the Safari browser. If you synch to Safari on a Macintosh or a Windows PC using iTunes, you can synch bookmarks, including the contents of your book-marks bar.

2. To open a bookmark, tap the Bookmarks button, and then press Folders to open them and Bookmarks to choose them.

3. To edit a bookmark or folder, tap the Bookmarks button, choose a folder or bookmark, and then press Edit. You can then press New Folder to create a new folder; press the Delete icon (red cir-cle) and choose Delete to delete it; drag the stacks icon to reposi-tion the item in its list; and edit the name or folder location by pressing the bookmark or folder.

4. To synch bookmarks with the Safari browser on a personal com-puter, connect iPad 2 to your personal computer. In iTunes, select iPad 2 in the sidebar. Click the Info tab, choose Other, Synch Safari bookmarks, and then click Apply.

Changing Settings

Safari has a moderate number of settings you can use to control its operation. Go to the Settings app on your iPad 2 and choose Safari to access them. The choices are as follows (see Figure 6.6):

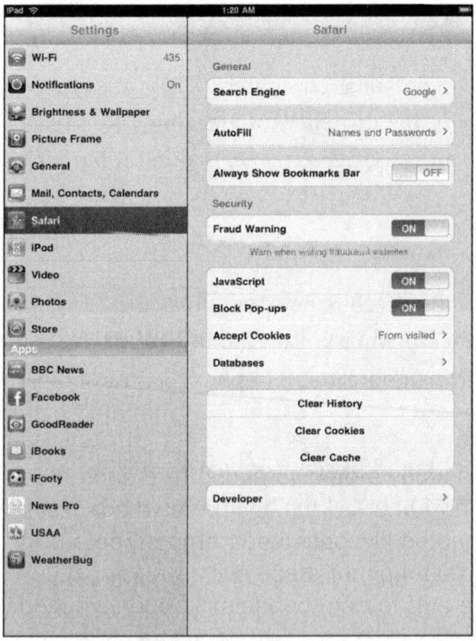

FIGURE 6.6　Safari settings can make your iPad 2 web life easier.

▸ **Search Engine**—Choose Google, Yahoo!, or Bing.

▸ **Autofill**—Choose this setting to use information from Contacts and specify which contact is your own personal information; also use this setting to turn on storage of names and passwords for various web pages.

▸ **Always Show Bookmarks Bar**—Slide to turn the display of the Bookmarks Bar on or off. The Bookmarks Bar is a useful convenience feature, but it takes up precious vertical screen space.

▸ **Fraud Warning**—Slide to turn warnings for potentially fraudulent websites on or off.

▶ **JavaScript**—Slide to turn JavaScript on or off. I recommend leaving JavaScript on so you get the functionality it provides, unless some websites start crashing or dramatically slowing your machine; in this case, try turning JavaScript off.

▶ **Block Pop-Ups**—Slide to block pop-ups. I recommend blocking them, as many ads are pop-ups, and who needs the distraction?

▶ **Accept Cookies**—Cookies are little files that a site places on your device to store information about you. The information can be for your benefit, such as preferences for using the website, or for the benefit of the people who run the site, such as information used to target specific kinds of ads to you. Slide to either accept all cookies, to accept cookies only from visited websites, or to not accept any cookies.

▶ **Databases**—With this setting, you can view the storage size of databases associated with web use, such as for Gmail or Google contacts.

▶ **Clear History, Cookies, Cache**—These options are useful for removing history information you'd rather keep private, or for trying to solve potential problems with system instability.

▶ **Developer**—Choose and slide to turn on the developer debug console to help you find and fix errors in a website you're developing.

As you use your iPad 2, you should find a decreasing number of sites that have multimedia content that doesn't work on iPad 2. However, this will be a work in progress for a long time to come. If the content you want to view is not accessible on iPad 2, you'll have to look for alternative approaches to getting the information you desire—such as visiting the site using a personal computer.

Summary

In this lesson, you learned how to use Apple's Safari web browser to surf the Web from your iPad 2, including using the iPad 2 in portrait and landscape modes, opening and navigating web pages, zooming and scrolling, using bookmarks, and changing settings. In the next lesson, you'll learn about creating and managing email on your iPad 2.

LESSON 7

Synching, Sending, and Receiving Email

In this lesson, you learn how to make your iPad 2 into a highly capable email machine. You find out how to access and synchronize multiple accounts, read and reply to messages, and create and send new messages. Additionally, you find out how to configure settings that manage how email works on your iPad 2.

Setting Up Email Accounts

One of the most promising uses for the iPad 2 is as a quick and easy-to-use email machine. You can use it for occasional keeping up, using a personal computer as your main email platform; in partnership with email on a smartphone such as the iPhone; or as your main email device. You can use a single email account; multiple accounts from Webmail providers, your employer, and other sources; and separate mail apps such as Gmail. Either way, using email with iPad 2 is flexible and fast.

Compare checking email on the iPad 2 to checking it on a personal computer. At home, the difference is simple: It takes literally a few seconds and a couple of screen presses on the iPad 2. (Which does this even faster than the original iPad did.) On a personal computer, it takes a couple of minutes, with mouse clicks and waits alternating throughout. The iPad 2 wins, no contest.

It's on the move, though, that the iPad really shows its email capabilities versus a PC. Getting an iPad rather than a personal computer out of your bag is far easier. And it's much easier and less obtrusive to take notes, check for new email messages, or write an email than on a personal computer. Sending, receiving, and making a quick check are all easy and convenient, not an anxious, major hassle. The screen size and onscreen keyboard are far more usable than what you can find on a smartphone. You have the capability to set up multiple email accounts on your iPad 2. You can then switch among them in the Mail app. iPad 2 can be a focal point for all your email, or whatever subset of your email you choose. However, if you choose MobileMe or Microsoft Exchange, only one account of either type can be your main resource for email, calendar, and contacts.

The iPad 2 directly supports MobileMe and Microsoft Exchange. For setting up access to a Microsoft Exchange account in an organizational setting, you should get help from your organization because specific details exist for your organization's Exchange setup that you can get only from the people who manage it.

TIP: **Using a Google Account on iPad 2**

If you have a Google account, set it up as a Microsoft Exchange account to use it as your main resource for email, calendar, and contacts. (If you use the Gmail option instead, you'll only get mail.) For information on setting up a Google account as your main account on your iPad 2, visit www.google.com/support/mobile/bin/answer.py?hl=en&answer=138740.

Make sure you have an active Internet connection. Then follow these steps to set up an account on iPad 2:

1. Choose Settings, Mail, Contacts, Calendars.

2. Tap the Add Account button.

3. Choose an account type: Microsoft Exchange, MobileMe, Gmail, Yahoo! Mail, AOL, or Other.

   MobileMe provides specific features for your iPad 2 and can be synchronized with other devices, such as an iPhone, Mac, or PC. Consider trying MobileMe, especially if you don't already have a central source for calendar and contacts to use with your iPad 2. For more information, visit www.apple.com/mobileme, shown in Figure 7.1.

FIGURE 7.1   MobileMe can keep you synched up.

4. Enter your account information and tap Save.

   In the event that you are lacking information needed for some of the fields, you can contact the service provider for your account or a help desk associate for your account, or you could access the Help files online.

   Your iPad 2 verifies your account information.

5. For a MobileMe account only, select the items you want to use on iPad 2: Mail, Contacts, Calendars, and Bookmarks.

6. For a Microsoft Exchange account only, select the items you want to use on iPad 2: Mail, Contacts, and Calendars.

   For Microsoft Exchange accounts, you can set the number of days of email to synchronize and which folders to push. For instance, you can push your entire Inbox, or just specific folders.

   You can set up a special folder on your Microsoft Exchange account and use various rules to send only some email, such as email from certain people that is more likely to be urgent, to that folder. (The emails can live only in that folder, or you can keep a copy in your account's Inbox as well.) You can then push only that folder to your iPad 2.

NOTE: **What *Push* Means for Email**

When discussing email, the term *push* refers to the ability of the email host to send, or push, new emails to your iPad 2 as soon as they're available—without you or your mail client software having to ask for new emails to be downloaded. Push means you get your email quicker.

If you have multiple accounts, specify which account will be used as your default account for sending mail. This can be done in Settings, as described later in this lesson.

TIP: **Google Accounts Synch Online**

You don't have to use iTunes to synch email, calendar, and/or contacts information from your Google account to your iPad 2; instead, information is synched over the Internet.

Reading Email

The Mail icon shows the number of unanswered emails in your Inbox from all accounts.

Follow these steps to check your mail:

1. Tap the Mail icon.

2. To change accounts, tap Inbox and then Accounts. Choose an account from the list.

   If the account's Inbox has not been updated by push email or by fetching, it will now update, if you have an active Internet connection.

3. Tap a folder—usually the Inbox, but you can choose other folders as well—to view the email messages in it.

4. To see more messages, scroll to the bottom of the list and tap Load More Messages.

If you have an active Internet connection, additional messages will load.

5. To delete an email in the message list, swipe left and right over it to see the Delete button, as shown in Figure 7.2. Tap the Delete button to delete the message. To delete multiple messages, tap Edit, select the messages to be deleted, and then tap Delete. (Or, to move messages, start by selecting the messages to move, and then tap Move. Select a mailbox or folder to move the messages to.)

FIGURE 7.2   iPad 2 Mail can display PDFs and many other types of files as attachments.

6. Tap a message description to read the message in full and act on it.

7. To better view the message, use gestures, as with Safari in the previous lesson: pinch to zoom; tap links to follow them; press and hold a link to see its destination address.

8. To view an attachment, tap it.

If you have an active Internet connection, the file downloads and, if the file type is supported by iPad 2, it displays, as shown in Figure 7.3. To save an image to your Photos album, tap it, and then choose Save Image. For other types of files, if you have an app that can open and potentially edit them, iPad 2 displays a button allowing you to do so. To clear the document from the screen, tap the screen, and then choose Done.

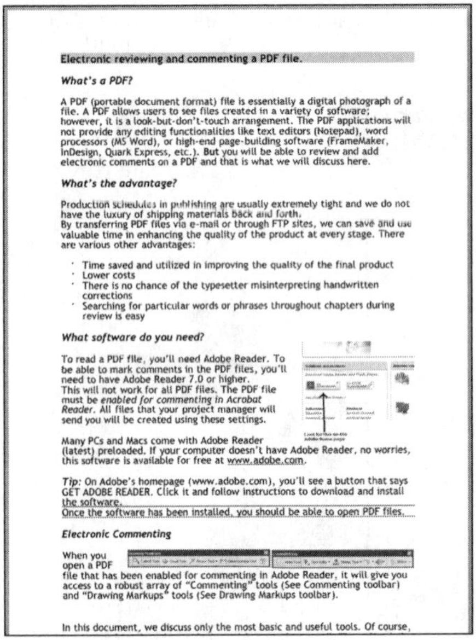

Electronic reviewing and commenting a PDF file.

What's a PDF?

A PDF (portable document format) file is essentially a digital photograph of a file. A PDF allows users to see files created in a variety of software; however, it is a look-but-don't-touch arrangement. The PDF applications will not provide any editing functionalities like text editors (Notepad), word processors (MS Word), or high-end page-building software (FrameMaker, InDesign, Quark Express, etc.). But you will be able to review and add electronic comments on a PDF and that is what we will discuss here.

What's the advantage?

Production schedules in publishing are usually extremely tight and we do not have the luxury of shipping materials back and forth.
By transferring PDF files via e-mail or through FTP sites, we can save and use valuable time in enhancing the quality of the product at every stage. There are various other advantages:

- Time saved and utilized in improving the quality of the final product
- Lower costs
- There is no chance of the typesetter misinterpreting handwritten corrections
- Searching for particular words or phrases throughout chapters during review is easy

What software do you need?

To read a PDF file, you'll need Adobe Reader. To be able to mark comments in the PDF files, you'll need to have Adobe Reader 7.0 or higher.
This will not work for all PDF files. The PDF file must be *enabled for commenting in Acrobat Reader*. All files that your project manager will send you will be created using these settings.

Many PCs and Macs come with Adobe Reader (latest) preloaded. If your computer doesn't have Adobe Reader, no worries, this software is available for free at www.adobe.com.

Tip: On Adobe's homepage (www.adobe.com), you'll see a button that says GET ADOBE READER. Click it and follow instructions to download and install the software.
Once the software has been installed, you should be able to open PDF files.

Electronic Commenting

When you open a PDF file that has been enabled for commenting in Adobe Reader, it will give you access to a robust array of "Commenting" tools (See Commenting toolbar) and "Drawing Markups" tools (See Drawing Markups toolbar).

In this document, we discuss only the most basic and useful tools. Of course,

FIGURE 7.3 iPad 2 Mail can display PDFs and many other types of files as attachments.

9. To act on the message, tap an icon to put it in a folder, to delete it, or to reply to it. (When you choose Reply, you also get the option to Reply All or to Forward the message.)

NOTE: **How to Search Email**

To search email, scroll to the top of your mailbox or tap the status bar to move quickly to the top. Enter text in the Search field. Tap

the fields you want to search: From, To, or the Subject. (You can't
search within the body of the email.) Begin the search; mail already
downloaded for the currently open account will be searched. If
available, tap Continue Search on Server to also search emails
stored on the server for your account.

10. To view the sender and other recipients of a message, and to have
additional options, tap the link, Details, at the top of the email
message.

11. Tap on a name to view details; the details then appear, as shown
in Figure 7.4. Tap the name to email the person; tap Create New
Contact or Add to Existing Contact to add the person's information to your Contacts.

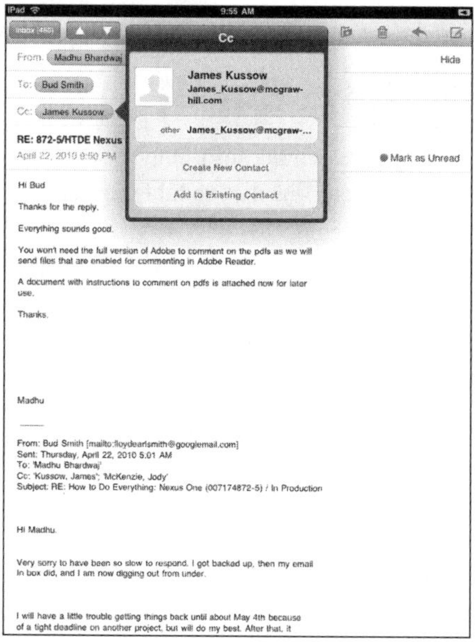

FIGURE 7.4 View another party's details and email them.

12. Tap Mark as Unread to mark the message as unread and prompt yourself to open it again, whether on iPad 2 or some other system. Tap Hide to hide the details.

NOTE: **How Attachment File Types Work**

For attachments, file types that iPad 2 can display include pictures (JPEG, GIF, and TIFF), which are displayed within the body of the email; audio files (MP3, Apple's AAC, WAV, and AIFF), which are played on request; and various kinds of office documents, including PDFs, web pages, plain text files, the iPad 2's own Pages, Keynote, and Numbers, and Microsoft's Word, Excel, and PowerPoint. Office documents are only viewable, not editable, unless you have specific software to do so. You should be able to select, copy, and paste text out of them, though. Also, you can't store the attachment in a folder, although you can find it again by finding the email message or by opening the app that you viewed or played the attachment with.

Creating and Sending Email

Sending email is easy, especially if you have contact information set up, making email addresses of your correspondents easily available to you. You have a lot of options. Follow these steps:

1. Tap the Compose icon.

2. In the To field, begin to type a name, or tap + to search for a name in your Contacts. Repeat for additional contacts.

If you type in the To field, matching names appear from email addresses you've used before and from your contacts. If you choose contacts, you can use search to hone in on a contact quickly. Both the To field and your contacts search as you type each character, so you may need to type only a couple of characters to get the email address you need, if it's one you've used before.

3. To add to the Cc: or Bcc: fields, or to change the From: address, tap the line showing the field to open it. Enter the additional email addresses, as shown in Figure 7.5. To change the From:

address, tap the current address, and then choose which of your email accounts to use from the list that appears.

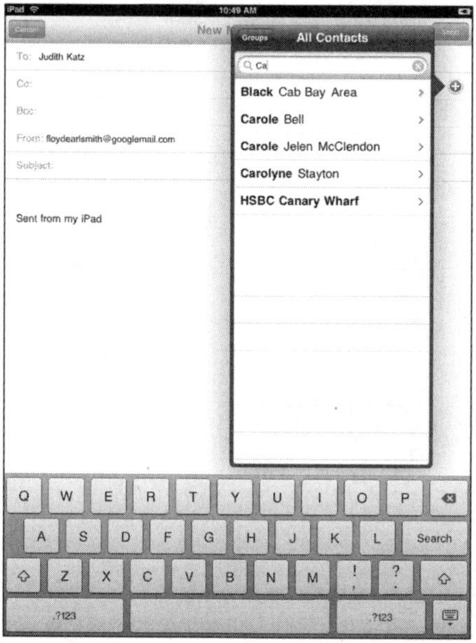

FIGURE 7.5 Pick a contact to send to.

4. Enter a subject and type your message.

   While entering a message, to save a draft, tap Cancel, and then tap Save. You can recover the message from the Drafts mailbox.

5. Tap Send.

This completes the process and sends your message.

Changing Mail Settings

Some email settings are set in the mail application or when configuring the account, as described earlier in this lesson. You can also use a number of settings in the Settings app to manage the display and functionality of all email Inboxes that you access through the iPad 2 Mail app, as shown in Figure 7.6:

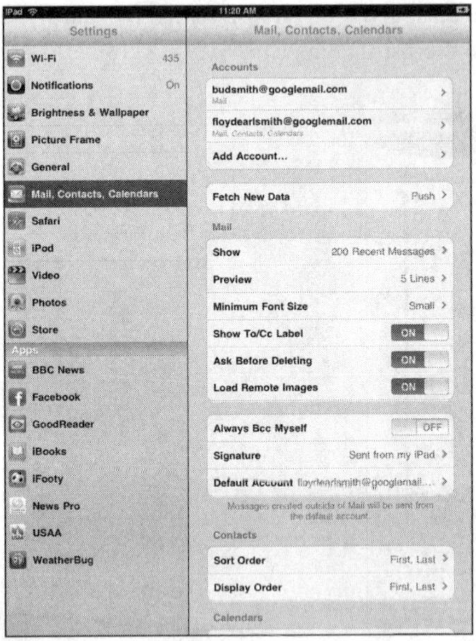

FIGURE 7.6   Mail settings bring your iPad 2 email to life.

▶ **Accounts**—This setting enables you to add, delete, and configure accounts.

▶ **Fetch New Data**—For accounts that do not push email, the Email app will fetch it. Choose a schedule for fetching. (Fetching less frequently saves battery life.)

▶ **Show Messages Number**—This setting enables you to specify how many recent messages to show without having to tap a button to load more messages.

▶ **Preview Lines, Font Size**—With this setting, you can specify the number of preview lines and the font size used in displaying the message list.

▶ **Show To/Cc Label, Ask Before Deleting, Load Remote Images**—You can turn these options on and off to control how iPad 2 works with individual emails.

> NOTE: **Fetching Instead of Pushing**
>
> If your email account doesn't push new emails out to you as they come in, your account can periodically request that any new emails be downloaded. This is called *fetching*.

▶ **Always Bcc Myself**—Turning on this setting will help you manage the emails you send or forward by always sending a blind carbon copy to yourself.

▶ **Signature**—With this setting, you can enter text to append to the bottom of each email, such as your name, email address, and phone number.

▶ **Default Account**—If you have multiple email accounts, you can specify which one to use for sending emails from other apps, such as the Notes app described in Lesson 8, "Using Contacts and Notes."

▶ **Contacts Sort**—Here you can specify the default sort order and display order for contacts.

▶ **Calendars**—This setting enables you to specify whether new invitations generate an alert, how far back to synchronize events, and which time zone to use for managing your events. (You should change the time zone when you travel across time zones, to avoid confusion.)

Summary

In this lesson, you learned how to set up email accounts on the iPad 2; how to read, create, and send email; and how to change email settings. In the next lesson, you learn how to use contacts—a key type of data for tying your personal organizational impact together—and notes.

LESSON 8

Using Contacts and Notes

In this lesson, you learn how to use your iPad 2 Contacts and Notes, and learn which apps will help you stay organized and in touch.

Setting Up Contacts

Keeping track of contacts has always been an effort. Millions of blank contacts books, Rolodexes for business cards, and other devices have been sold just for this purpose. Today, with more ways to reach people than ever, contacts information is even more important.

The iPad 2 is a great device for working with contacts. The large screen, easy portability, and ease of use help to make it ideal for capturing and exchanging information. It's easy to look things up on iPad 2 and to fill out contact information. After you enter the contact information, it's also easy to email people (see the previous lesson), pull up a number to call them, or integrate an address into a note. To add a great deal more power, the iPad 2 makes it easy to share contact information with your other devices.

> TIP: **Faces "Make" Facebook**
>
> There are many reasons why Facebook is one of the most popular online services around, but one of them has to be the sheer power of "putting a face to a name" online. Similarly, it's surprising how much using photos on your contact's information brings them to life. When you set out to contact someone using their photo, you're using the more social side of your brain, recognizing faces rather than reading words. Try to find time to associate photos with all your contacts; it makes picking people out for sending emails or setting up meetings easier and more fun.

Creating or Updating a Contact

Even if you get contacts onto your iPad 2 by synchronizing them from an existing contacts list, you will still occasionally need to enter contacts directly onto your iPad 2. Also, a quick look at the process makes you more aware of what the potential fields are, helping you do a better job of capturing relevant information and synching what you capture across platforms.

TIP: **Get Information Together First**

Because the iPad 2 offers limited multitasking, it's often helpful to try to handle subtasks (such as getting a photo for someone) before starting the overall task (such as creating a new contact for that person). Try to have contact information (such as email addresses, address information, and so on) at hand, and have a photo ready in the Photo app (see Lesson 12, "Getting Apps from the App Store") before creating or modifying a contact, or you may have to start over—perhaps even several times. Consider consolidating the relevant textual information in a note, as described at the end of this lesson, pasting it into the Notes field of a contact, and then cutting and pasting each part of that into the appropriate field of a contact.

Follow these steps to create a new contact:

   1. Consider which photo you want to use for the person, business, and so on, and bring that photo into an easy-to-find place in your Photo Album.

TIP: **Use Photos and Screenshots, Too**

In place of a photo for a business contact, consider using a screenshot of their business from Street View in the Maps app. You can do the same for teachers (use their school) and friends (use their house). For real photos of people, Facebook is a good source. See Lesson 11 for working with maps and Lesson 13 for working with photos and other images, including screenshots.

   2. Press the Contacts app to start it.

Figure 8.1 shows a completed contact for reference.

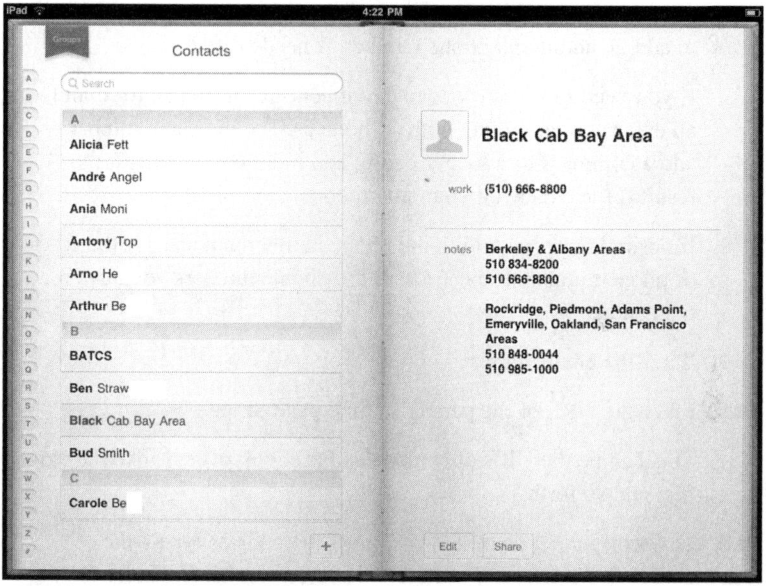

FIGURE 8.1 Make your Contacts as complete as possible.

3. Press the + button to add a contact.

4. Press Add Photo to add a photo.

A list of photo albums appears. You also have the option of taking a picture with the built-in camera, as described in Chapter 13.

5. Pick out the photo you want by pressing it.

The photo will be added to the contact.

6. Enter the first name, last name, and/or company name for the contact.

7. Specify the type of phone number. If the default (mobile) is correct, there's no need to change it. However, if it's a different type of phone number, press the word "mobile." A list of alternatives will appear, including mobile, home, work, home fax, work fax, pager, assistant, car, company main, and radio. Choose the most appropriate descriptor.

8. Enter the phone number of the type specified.

As you add the phone number, a field opens up beneath it for you to add an additional phone number, if needed.

If you need to add a pause to a number—for instance, for dialing an extension, or dialing with a phone card or discount number— add a comma. For a longer pause, add more commas. Test the result for accuracy on your smartphone.

9. If desired, enter an additional phone number and specify the type of phone number. Repeat for all the phone numbers you have for the contact.

10. Enter the email address.

11. Enter the URL of the person's home page, if any.

This can be the URL of someone's Facebook page, LinkedIn profile, and so forth.

12. To specify the type of address, press the address type—the default is Home—and choose the appropriate label: Home, Work, or Other. Then enter the address, if any.

Enter the street address, city, state, and ZIP code. If the country isn't the U.S., press the country name and then choose the correct country from the scrolling list that appears. As with phone numbers, you can add additional addresses of various types.

> NOTE: **Enter Full International Addresses**
> U.S.-style addresses are quite simple compared to some other countries, which tend to include house names, street names, county names, and so on. If a mailing address is too complex to simplify into the Contacts address block, consider entering it into the Notes field.

13. If desired, enter Notes—this can be any information you want to remember about the person.

14. To add more information, click the + next to Add field. Then choose a field from the list, as shown in Figure 8.2. Fields available

include Prefix (such as Mr., Mrs., Miss, and so on), Phonetic
First Name or Phonetic Last Name, Middle Name, Suffix (such
as Esq. for an attorney), Nickname, Job Title, Department,
Instant Message address, Birthday date, and Date (intended to be
used for remembering an anniversary or similar type of date).

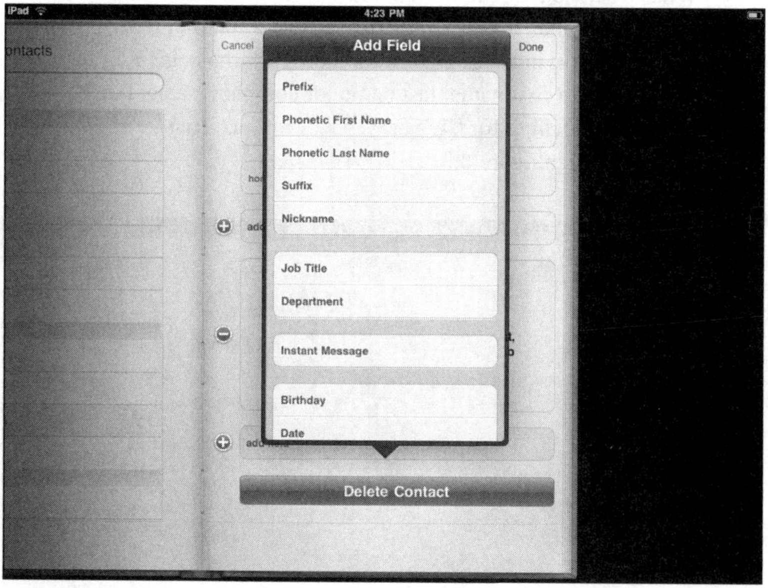

FIGURE 8.2   Additional fields can be added to your contacts.

Searching and Updating Contacts

When searching for contacts, you can search only by first name, last name,
or company name. However, you'll find that sometimes you'll enter a
search string, such as "An," and have contact names appear that don't
begin with "An."

The reason you see additional contacts in the search results is that the
search includes the company name associated with the contact. However,
the company name is not displayed in search results if there is also a person's name, which leads to your getting some search results that don't visibly match your search string.

For instance, a search for "An" will bring up people named "Andy," but also people of any name who work for "An Enormous Company"—but not people who work for "A Rich and Enormous Company."

Use these tips to help you with searching in contacts:

▶ When you use the search function, the onscreen keyboard automatically capitalizes the first letter. Whether the first letter is capitalized or not, matches are returned only for the beginning of a word within a first name, last name, or company name. For instance, searching for "Tr" or "tr" will return "Trish" but not "Patricia." See Figure 8.3.

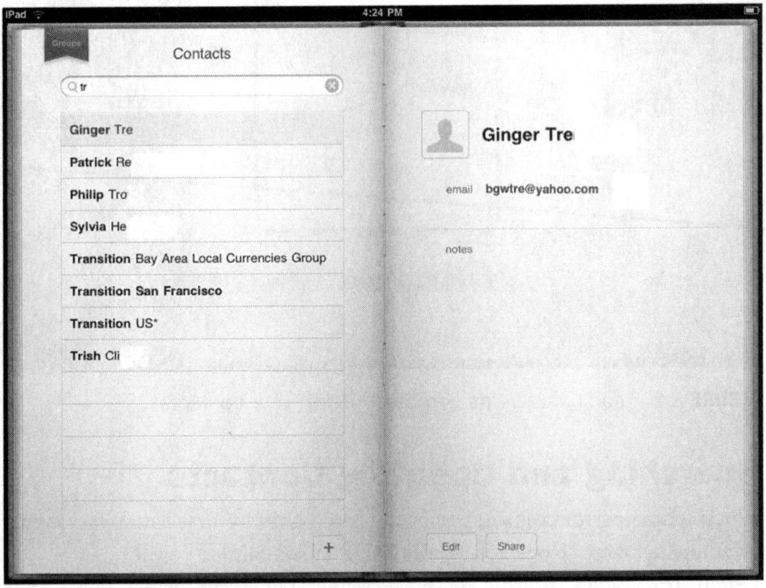

FIGURE 8.3   Searching with all lowercase letters matches within words.

▶ For Exchange accounts only, to search an enterprise Global Address List (GAL), tap Groups and then the Exchange server name. Although search will work, you will not have the capability to edit contacts you find, nor will you be able to save them to the iPad 2.

▶ Also for Exchange accounts only, to search a Lightweight Directory Access Protocol (LDAP) server, tap Groups and then the LDAP server name. As mentioned in the previous search option, although you can search for a contact, you won't be able to edit them or save them to the iPad 2.

Synching Contacts

You can bring in contacts from other platforms and share the contact information that you create or edit on iPad 2 in several ways:

▶ Use a MobileMe, Microsoft Exchange, or other host as your main source for email, calendar, and/or contacts information (see the previous lesson).

▶ Use iTunes to synch contacts from Google, Yahoo!, or with applications on your computer (see Lesson 11, "Working with Maps").

▶ Have your organization help you access internal contacts directories by setting up an Exchange account with contacts enabled, or an LDAP account. Access to such accounts is read-only; you can't edit contacts you access from Exchange or LDAP, nor can you save these contacts to your iPad 2. This reduces the usefulness of having the contacts available somewhat, because you can't update them with new information.

Creating and Sharing Notes

The Notes app may just be one of the best uses of the iPad 2 as a kind of super-powered version of a paper notebook. Compared to a paper notebook, using the Notes app on iPad 2 has many advantages, including these:

▶ **More flexible**—In addition to Notes, other apps are available to you on the iPad 2, and with a Wi-Fi iPad 2, you can connect to the Internet in many places where you might be taking notes; with an iPad 2 Wi-Fi+3G, you can connect to the Internet from nearly anywhere.

▶ **Sharable**—You can easily email notes, which makes them a great option for sharing the proceedings of meetings and so on, and synch them with some email applications, such as Microsoft Outlook (see Lesson 18, "Using iTunes and Home Sharing").

▶ **Searchable**—You can search the titles of notes on iPad 2 and the entire contents of notes when you send them to an application on the iPad 2 (such as the Pages app available on iPad 2) or on a personal computer.

The Notes app has two main features: the list of notes and individual notes. In the next two sections, I show you how to create an individual note and then show you all the things you can do with a note after you've created it.

Creating a Note

Follow these steps to create a Note:

1. Press the Notes app to start it.

2. Press the + button to create a note.

3. Enter the name of the note on the first line. Only about 20 characters will reliably display in the list of notes that you've written. (The number of characters displayed fluctuates, depending on the day or date that the iPad 2 displays next to the note name, as well as on word breaks and the width of specific characters.)

4. Type the note. The note that appears will be similar to the one shown in Figure 8.4. Typing speed and ease are very important in note taking. One helpful feature is to end each sentence with two spaces; the iPad 2 will insert a full stop and a single space, and then start the next sentence with a single capital letter.

TIP: **Save Keystrokes on Punctuation**
The only punctuation characters available on the initial iPad 2 onscreen keyboard are the comma, full stop, and (with shifting) the

exclamation point and question mark. Consider using a kind of punctuation shorthand, such as lots of ellipses (...) instead of dashes, and spelling out numbers instead of using digits, so you don't have to keep switching back and forth between the alphabetic keyboard, the numeric version, and the special characters version.

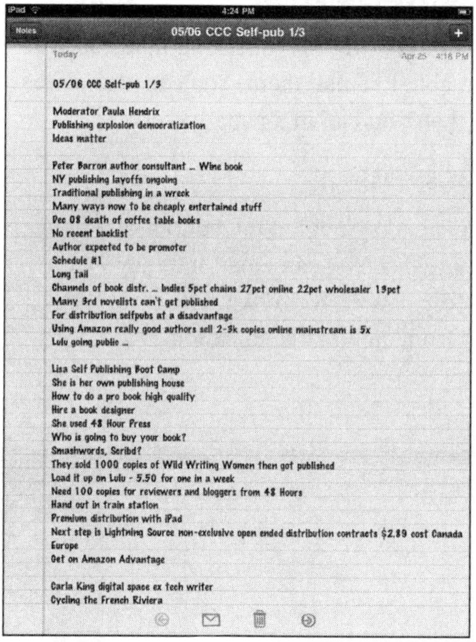

FIGURE 8.4 Use notes to record events, your thoughts, and more.

5. Press the keyboard key on the onscreen keyboard to make the onscreen keyboard go away so you can examine the note more easily.

6. You can edit the note at any time, and at any point. Press anywhere on the note to place the insertion point there and to bring up the onscreen keyboard. Make your changes as needed.

TIP: **Abbreviate Names to Fit**

Only the first 20 characters or so of the note's name will be visible in the list of notes, so consider using some kind of abbreviated naming convention for your notes. I start most of my notes with the date of creation, a short description of the place (such as "CCC" for the Commonwealth Club of California), and then a distinguishing word or two about the event or meeting.

Emailing and Managing Notes

One of the great advantages of using your iPad 2 for taking notes, instead of using a pen and paper, is being able to email them. You can also store many more notes on your iPad 2 than you can in a paper notebook.

Tips for using notes include the following:

▶ **To email a note**—Press the email symbol at the bottom of a note to email it, as shown in Figure 8.5. You can email it to anyone interested, or email it only to yourself, for forwarding from the Mail app on your iPad 2 or from an email application or service on a personal computer.

FIGURE 8.5 Email your notes to anyone interested in them.

▶ **To see note names**—Press the Notes button. In portrait mode, the list of names of notes is hidden.

▶ **To read through notes**—Use the arrow keys to move through notes, or press on note titles in the list of notes to move among them.

▶ **To search notes**—Use the Search field (in landscape mode) or press the Notes button (in portrait mode). Enter characters one at a time to build up your search string. As you enter each character, iPad 2 will display the list of notes whose names include the string of all the characters you've entered.

▶ **To delete a note**—Press the trash can to delete the note. (It's not necessary to delete notes to try to free up a large amount of storage capacity on your iPad 2; notes are quite small compared to songs and, especially, video. A gigabyte of storage on your iPad 2 can hold about one million notes, 300 songs, or one movie.)

▶ **To manage your notes by date**—Be aware of the following information: Notes are listed by the date of last modification. If you want to store the date on which your note was created, you have to include it in the note itself. (It might be helpful to put the date of creation in the titles of your notes, so you still have a record of the date of the event even if you edit the note later.)

▶ **To synch notes**—See Lesson 18, which explains how to synch notes with certain applications using iTunes.

CAUTION: **Watch Out for Shortened Notes**

The notes you create in the Notes app can be much larger than, for example, the Notes supported by Microsoft Outlook. If you use iTunes to synch your notes with Microsoft Outlook or another personal information management platform, check carefully to see just how much information gets through without truncation before counting on this method of transferring information.

Note that information is easily lost in the following ways:

▶ **A copy on a target platform**—When you synchronize a long iPad 2 note with another application that supports shorter notes, you lose information on the synched copy due to its being truncated on the other platform.

▶ **The iPad 2-based original**—If you edit a truncated note on another platform, the truncated note becomes the newer copy. When you synch the iPad 2 with the other platform, the longer version of the note you have stored on the iPad 2 is replaced in favor of the newer version that was first truncated, and then edited, on the other platform.

Summary

In this lesson, you learned how to use Contacts and Notes on the iPad 2. In the next lesson, you learn how to use the Calendar app as another part of staying organized.

LESSON 9

Getting the Most Out of the Calendar

In this lesson, you learn how to update, view, and synchronize your calendar, and receive alerts from it in a timely way to help you get things done.

How the Calendar Helps

Being where you need to be, when you need to be there, is an ongoing challenge for people everywhere. Because it's so portable, so easy to use, and so well integrated with other apps such as email and maps, the iPad 2 works very well as a personal organizational tool. It also "plays well with others," sharing events and updates with mobile phones and personal computers.

The calendar is a crucial part of staying organized, and a great thing to have with you "on the go." The iPad 2 is particularly well-suited for calendar use because of its large screen, letting you see lots of information at once, and without having to hassle with a laptop.

> TIP: **Synchronize Calendars**
> To synch calendars, use the iPad 2 preferences panel in iTunes (see Lesson 18, "Using iTunes and Home Sharing"), or turn on Calendars in your iPad 2 Settings for synching with a Microsoft Exchange or MobileMe account (see Lesson 7, "Synching, Sending, and Receiving Email").

Viewing Your Calendar

Viewing what's on your calendar is something you do just about every day, and the calendar is much more useful if you can make changes and additions as needed. The calendar on your iPad 2 has some real strengths in this regard:

▶ **Size and attractiveness**—The large screen size and the attractive appearance of your iPad 2's display make it great for managing calendar entries compared with, for instance, a mobile phone.

▶ **Portability**—You can easily take your iPad 2 with you so that you have your calendar entries—and the ability to add to or update them—close at hand.

▶ **Interactivity**—Your iPad 2 displays alerts on the home screen, even when it is otherwise inert, and it is easy to use for updating events and adding new information (see information on adding events later in this lesson).

▶ **Integration**—Your iPad 2 calendar can reflect information stored in other calendars and can be updated by entries made on other platforms (see the Tip about synching calendars).

CAUTION: **Don't Knock Your iPad 2**

At this writing, for reasons unknown, you can't swipe to move to the next or previous page of the calendar. Don't knock your iPad 2 off its stand trying to do so! Instead, use the date timeline at the bottom of the screen to change pages.

Here's how to view your calendar:

1. Tap the Calendar app to start it.

The calendar then appears, as shown in Figure 9.1.

2. If you have multiple calendars set up, tap the Calendars button and then select a calendar. Tap All Calendars to select them all.

3. Tap buttons on the top of the screen to move among Day, Week, Month, and List views.

All the views are useful, and you can switch from portrait to landscape mode to see which one you prefer for each view. The List view, shown in Figure 9.2, is a great combination of a scrollable list of events on the left and an easy-to-use, hour-by-hour view of the current day on the right.

FIGURE 9.1   Your calendar shows your events at a glance.

FIGURE 9.2   If it's in the List view, it probably won't be missed.

4. Tap buttons on the bottom of the screen to move to a different day, week, or month, depending on the current view.

5. Use the arrow keys to move one day, week, or month at a time.

6. Tap a time period to move to it, or tap on the left or right arrows to slide backward or forward in time.

   As you tap the arrows, the time period you're currently moving over displays onscreen. The main calendar display doesn't change until you stop dragging. When you move away from the current time period, the time period displayed is highlighted by a white box, whereas the current day, week, or month remains highlighted with a blue highlight.

7. Tap the Today button to return to the current day, week, or month.

TIP: **How to Search Calendar Items**

Searches of Calendar entries apply only to the title of an event, the location, and the name(s) of people invited—not to notes and other fields. To search, enter the word or words to search in the Search field; as you enter text, matching events appear in a list below. Click Search to move the keyboard away and view the complete results list.

Creating a Calendar Event

Many of your calendar events may come from entries made on other devices, such as a laptop or smartphone. However, you will likely want to enter, update, and, in many cases, share information directly from the iPad 2 as well.

Follow these steps to add a calendar event:

1. Move the calendar to the time period in which you want to make a new entry, to check that the time is available. (Refer to the "Viewing your Calendar" section found earlier in this lesson for details.)

2. Tap the + button in the lower-right corner of the calendar. The Add Event entry area appears, as shown in Figure 9.3.

FIGURE 9.3   Add events to stay up to date.

TIP: **From Email to Calendar**

If you receive event information in text form—for instance, in an email—copy it out of the email and then paste it into the Notes area of a new event. Then you can copy and paste information in the Notes area into the corresponding fields of the calendar event.

3. Enter the event title. The title should have easily recognized key words up front when looking at a shrunken view, as in the Month view on iPad 2, or for any view on a mobile phone.

4. Enter the location of the event. For maximum usability with your iPad 2's Maps app, or similar apps on other platforms, consider entering only the street address (such as 435 Post St, San Francisco). You can put the building name and other useful address information in the Notes.

   Also consider getting any directions that you need now and entering them in the Notes area for use on the way to the appointment.

5. Tap the Starts/Ends area to enter the start and end time, or use the All-day slider to indicate an all-day event.

6. Enter the starting and ending time using the date and time indicators. Unlike some other scheduling tools, you can specify times to the nearest five minutes, not just to the nearest quarter hour or half hour.

   To take travel times into account, you can either lengthen the event to include the travel times, create separate entries for the journey, or simply remember to account for it by using care when scheduling adjacent calendar events. Consider creating a policy for yourself that fits your needs, such as not noting journey times of 10 minutes or less, but creating separate entries for journey times of 15 minutes or more. Using separate entries is particularly useful for potentially complicated or important events, such as traveling to the airport for a trip or driving to a job interview.

7. Tap Repeat if the event recurs over time. You can choose to repeat the event every day, week, two weeks, month, or year. Certain more sophisticated choices, such as the last Friday of every month, are not available to be specified in Calendar.

8. Tap Invitees to enter people to invite.

TIP: **Use Calendar Invitations**

Consider making it a habit to invite people to an event using your calendar. That way, they not only are reminded of the event when it's created, but they can be automatically kept up to date with any changes as well.

9. Tap Alert to specify when the alert for the event will appear—in 5 minutes, 15 minutes, 30 minutes, 1 hour, 2 hours, 1 day, 2 days, or on the date of the event. (You will get the opportunity to enter a second alert as well.) Use a time period—or time periods, if you set up travel time and the actual event separately—that will allow for both travel to the event and preparation for it.

NOTE: **Alerts Appear Everywhere**

When you reach the time specified by the Alert for an event, an alert appears onscreen. Alerts appear even if you are on the Lock screen that appears when you start your iPad 2.

10. Tap Availability to show how the event appears in your calendar—busy, free, tentative, or out of office. This kind of busy/free notification is particularly useful if others are using your calendar to create events for you, or for including you in their event planning.

11. Tap Notes to enter notes about the event. Use the Notes section to organize and store related information about the event.

12. Tap Done to record the event. The event will then appear in your Calendar.

TIP: **Use the Calendar for To-Dos**

The Calendar app can be used as a to-do list. You can create all-day events or time-specific events. Alternatively, you might consider using one of the many To Do list manager apps available in the App Store.

CAUTION: **Watch Out for Time Zones**

The iPad 2 does not necessarily update the time for you when you are traveling through different time zones. Use the Date & Time settings (see Lesson 5, "Customizing General Settings for Your iPad 2") to update the time when you travel.

Responding to Meeting Invitations

You can receive meeting invitations only if you have a Microsoft Exchange account on your iPad 2 with Calendars enabled (see Lesson 7, "Synching, Sending, and Receiving Email"). If you receive an invitation, follow these steps:

1. Find the meeting invitation in the calendar, or the event notification in the In tray icon in the corner of your screen. The meeting invitation looks very similar to a new meeting, as shown in Figure 9.3.

2. To view contact information for the meeting organizer, tap Invitation From. Tap the email address to send the organizer an email message.

3. To view contact information for invitees, tap Invitees. Tap an invitee's name to see the contact information. Tap the email address to send the invitee an email message.

4. To set an alert, tap Alert and specify the alert time.

5. To add a comment, tap Add Comments and enter your comments.

   Comments appear in the Info screen for the meeting and may be visible to all participants.

6. To respond to the invitation, tap Accept, Maybe, or Decline. Add comments for the meeting organizer if desired, and then tap Done.

NOTE: **More Email Help**

You may receive meeting invitations by email instead of in your calendar. Open the email message and respond as indicated to accept or decline the invitation.

Subscribing to Calendars

Subscribing to a calendar allows calendar events from other calendars to appear on yours. You can't edit the entries or create new events for those calendars.

You can subscribe to a wide range of calendars, including Yahoo!, Google, and Macintosh iCal calendars. Any calendar that uses the CalDAV or iCalendar, or .ics, format will work. (Yahoo!, Google, and iCal calendars support both.)

The iPad 2 accepts invitations from iCalendar accounts, but not CalDAV accounts.

Follow these instructions to subscribe to a calendar:

1. Tap the Settings application icon.

2. Choose Mail, Contacts. Tap Calendar.

3. Tap Add Account, and then choose Other.

4. Choose Add Subscribed Calendar, for an iCalendar account, or Add CalDAV account.

5. Enter the account information.

6. Tap Next to verify the account.

7. Tap Save.

Summary

In this lesson, you learned how to view your calendar, create events, subscribe to calendars, and respond to meeting invitations. In the next lesson, I introduce using FaceTime for video phone calls and videoconferencing.

LESSON 10

Using FaceTime

In this lesson, you learn to use the built-in FaceTime app in conjunction with your front-facing camera to make video phone calls; then you learn to use the rear-facing camera option to show the view from your location.

Understanding FaceTime

The idea of video phone calls has captured the imagination for decades. From early science fiction stories, to the detective Dick Tracy's wristwatch video phones, and science fiction TV shows and movies, people have known this is the way we should communicate.

Today, the video phone call is a widespread reality. At the low end, you have free Skype video calls, conducted in a little window on a personal computer. At the high end are Cisco telepresence rooms that make people thousands of miles apart feel as if they share a conference room, at a cost of many thousands of dollars.

In many ways, Apple's FaceTime is the best of both worlds. It's free—the camera, the software, and the service are all included with any new Mac, the latest iPhone models, and of course the iPad 2. FaceTime on the iPad 2 is shown in Figure 10.1.

The quality is great. The front-facing camera on the iPad 2 has a resolution of "only" 640×480, which is not much for a digital camera but quite large for videoconferencing. The picture from FaceTime is updated at a very high rate of 30 frames per second, and it looks rock solid onscreen. (Optimizing around a fixed, moderate resolution allows FaceTime to provide really good performance most of the time.)

FaceTime also makes it easy to share your surroundings. The rear-facing camera on the iPad 2 is not that great for taking pictures, but it's excellent to use as a "show me" function during a video conference call.

FIGURE 10.1   FaceTime really shines on calls from one iPad 2 to another.

You might begin a FaceTime call to a friend by wishing her a happy birth-day. Then, switch to the rear-facing camera and pan around to family, friends, or co-workers to make it a virtual party.

Part of the reason FaceTime works so well is that the iPad 2 is a personal device. The iPad 2 combines true portability, and a size that allows you to hold it comfortably, along with a big screen that FaceTime keeps filled with, well, your face. The effect is very "in your face," in a good way. You really do get more out of the conversation.

FaceTime is also the best video conferencing tool for iPhones and Macs, but iPhones are quite small, and Macs are not that portable. With its face-size screen and high portability, the iPad 2 is perfect for FaceTime.

The only problem with FaceTime is that not everyone can get it—and you can't use it all the time. FaceTime works only on Wi-Fi connections, not on cell phone connections. So you can't use it when you're out and about if you depend on a 3G connection in your iPad 2. But you can use FaceTime when if you connect to a wireless network, which includes times when you tether to a portable hot spot provided by your iPhone 4 or other smartphone.

In addition, FaceTime doesn't work on Windows PCs or any kind of mobile phone except the latest iPhone models—and it doesn't interoperate with other systems. Consider using an alternative video phone call service, such as Skype, for friends who don't have FaceTime.

> **NOTE: Who Wants to Do a Video Call?**
>
> Don't be surprised if your friends, family members, and business colleagues who haven't been spoiled by FaceTime's reliability and quality are not as excited about the idea of doing a video call as you are. Most people haven't grown up with the idea, and are often quite concerned about how they look onscreen. Once people try it, though, they tend to like it a lot.

So FaceTime is currently excellent among people who can use it—people who have a Mac, iPhone 4, or iPad 2. However, that's a minority of people. Perhaps someday, FaceTime and other videoconferencing tools will interoperate, giving people more flexibility. Until then, the utility of FaceTime is limited to a lucky few.

> **NOTE: Why Are the Cameras So Cheap?**
>
> On the one hand, people admire the way Apple provides thoughtfully integrated hardware, software, and online connectivity—but then they criticize the company for things like the front-facing camera on the iPad 2. The thing is, the camera is there for FaceTime. If the camera were higher-resolution, there would be a lot more data to stream, and a lot more likelihood of dropped frames, dropped calls, and other problems. The same goes, to a lesser extent, to the rear-facing camera that you can also easily use with FaceTime. Apple wasn't being cheap by integrating low-end camera sensors; the company was also supporting a strong overall user experience.

Setting Up FaceTime

FaceTime uses your email address for making FaceTime calls between people. There's no phone number, just email addresses.

> **NOTE: Check Email Addresses Before You FaceTime**
>
> Check with the people you want to talk to on FaceTime beforehand to find out what email address to use—it may not be the email address that you have for them. Likewise, provide people with the email address they should use to reach you on FaceTime—or add

every single one of your email addresses to your FaceTime settings, as described in this section, so that no one uses the
"wrong" one.

To set up FaceTime before you start to use it, follow these steps:

1. From the home panel of the Home screen, tap Settings.

The Settings screen appears.

2. Tap FaceTime.

The FaceTime settings screen appears, requesting your Apple ID,
as shown in Figure 10.2.

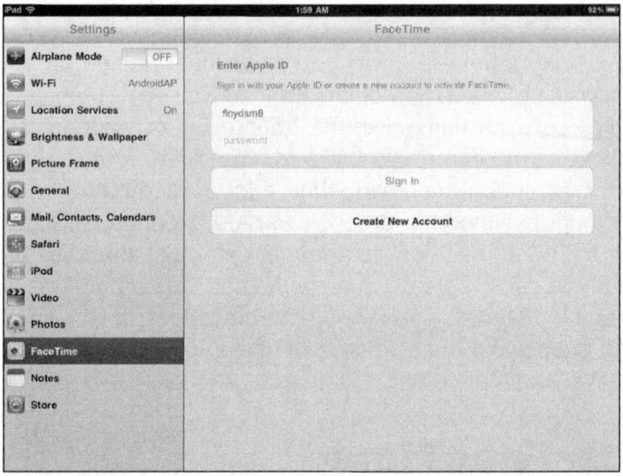

FIGURE 10.2   Use your Apple ID to sign in to FaceTime.

3. If you don't have an Apple ID, tap Create New Account, and follow the steps shown to create one. Otherwise, skip to Step 4.

4. Enter your user name and password. Tap Sign In.

You're signed in to FaceTime.

5. Enter the email address you wish to use as a "handle" for FaceTime calls. Tap Verify. If requested, check your email Inbox and follow the instructions in the FaceTime email you are sent.

Apple verifies the email address. You are presented with the FaceTime Settings screen, shown in Figure 10.3.

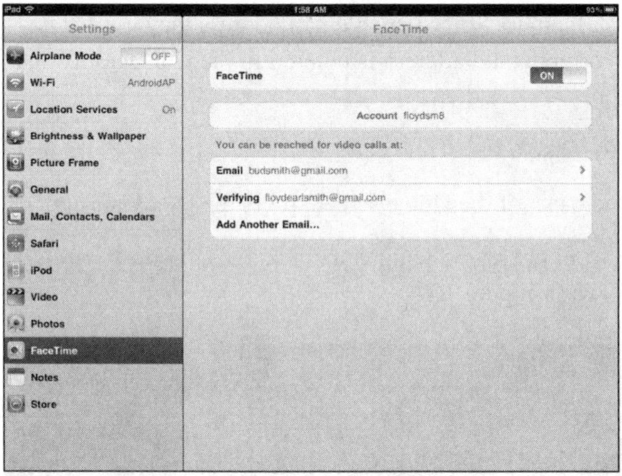

FIGURE 10.3   You can turn FaceTime on and off, and add more email addresses.

6. To turn FaceTime off, so that no one can call you, turn the FaceTime slider to Off.

7. To add an email address, tap Add Another Email, and follow the onscreen instructions.

Making a Call with FaceTime

The easiest way to get to know FaceTime is by making a call with it—or a few calls. Before you start, you need the following:

▶ Your iPad 2

▶ Access to a Wi-Fi connection

▶ One or more friends with an iPad 2, an iPhone 4, or a Macintosh with a camera

▶ A contact set up in advance for each friend you want to call, containing the email address that the contact uses for FaceTime

You may need to contact friends ahead of time to find out if they use FaceTime, and to ask them to verify which email address they use for it. Make sure that the correct email address is entered in the Contact information on your iPad.

Follow these steps to make a FaceTime call:

1. From the home panel of the Home screen, press the FaceTime app.

A live image from the front-facing camera and a sign-in screen appear, as shown in Figure 10.4.

FIGURE 10.4 FaceTime asks you to sign in.

2. To learn more about FaceTime and your iPad 2, click the link, Learn More About FaceTime.

Information about FaceTime, other built-in apps, and your iPad 2 appears, as shown in Figure 10.5.

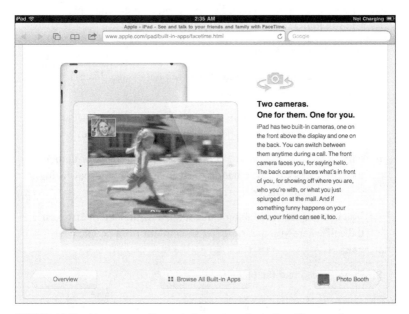

FIGURE 10.5 You can easily get information about FaceTime and more.

If you want to return to this screen later, the URL is www.apple.com/ipad/built-in-apps/facetime.html.

3. To return to FaceTime, double-tap the Home button; then choose FaceTime from among the currently running apps on display.

4. Sign in to your Apple account, or create a new one, to use FaceTime. To use an existing account, enter your password and tap Sign In. To create a new account, tap Create New Account. Enter your first name, last name, password, security question, and country or region. Tap in the check box to Subscribe or choose not to subscribe to news, special offers, and information about related products and services. Tap Next when finished.

You're signed into your existing or new account.

5. Enter the email address people should use to call you. Press Next. If FaceTime sends a verification email to the address you entered, respond to it.

   The email address is verified. Your contacts appear.

6. Choose the contact to call. For that contact, press the email address to use.

   FaceTime tries to connect.

7. If the call does not go through, you see a message: FaceTime Failed. Click OK and try again.

   If the call does go through, the view from your friend's iPad fills the screen. Your image appears in a corner of the screen.

8. During the call, press the Microphone button to mute or unmute the call. Press the Swap button to swap between the front-facing and rear-facing cameras.

   You can use the rear-facing camera to show the other person on the call where you are, or to get a shout out from people near you.

9. Press End to end the call.

You may need to contact friends ahead of time to find out if they use FaceTime, and to ask them to verify which email address(es) they use for it. Make sure that the correct email address for FaceTime is entered in the Contact information on your iPad.

Summary

In this lesson, you learned to use the front-facing camera and the built-in FaceTime app to make video phone calls, and to use the rear-facing camera to show the person you're talking to the view from your location. In the next lesson, you learn how to use the Maps app for directions, finding different kinds of businesses nearby, and more.

LESSON 11

Working with Maps

In this lesson, you learn what to expect from the location services and Maps app for either a Wi-Fi-only iPad 2 or a 3G unit. You also learn how to use the Maps app to find your current location, get directions, use Street View and other views, get traffic updates, and more.

Getting the Most Out of Maps

Mapping on the iPad 2 is full of capabilities and possibilities. The size and direct tactile input of the iPad 2 are very well suited for use with online mapping, and the maps displayed look spectacular. There are some complexities as well, however, especially if you have a Wi-Fi-only iPad 2.

> CAUTION: **Online Maps Aren't Perfect**
>
> Online maps are constructed from a wide range of different data sources with varying degrees of age and accuracy. Don't be too surprised if you're told to drive the wrong way on a one-way street, or to take a long walk on a short pier, or to cross an international border to visit the drugstore—and be sure you have the street smarts to know when you shouldn't follow directions! Look carefully at the suggestions given, and double-check any directions that seem dubious.

Using a 3G iPad 2

The 3G models of the iPad 2 have built-in GPS hardware, located in the same hardware module as the 3G circuitry, offering you almost everything you could want for GPS. On a 3G iPad 2, you have the following:

▶ **a-GPS location support**—a-GPS means "assisted GPS," and it's the best way to have an accurate location fix nearly all the time.

a-GPS is the best kind of GPS: You're connected to GPS satellites circling high overhead nearly all of the time (the "GPS" part); when you're not, the iPad 2 uses nearby cell towers and Wi-Fi network base stations to figure out your location (the "a-" part). a-GPS includes cell towers in its location calculations even if you aren't currently on a data plan.

When starting up navigation services, a-GPS gets a quick fix from cell towers and Wi-Fi base station locations first, then uses the satellites when they finish downloading their data—which happens up to a minute later. Because you have either satellite visibility or cell tower accessibility, or both, nearly all of the time, you also have a good location nearly all of the time.

▶ **Data connection for maps**—Knowing your location is great, but you need a data connection to download map data so the Maps application can keep up with you. With a 3G iPad, you nearly always have a data connection, so you almost always have fresh map data when you need it.

▶ **Directions**—The iPad 2 Maps app gives you very useful directions. However, it does not provide live, turn-by-turn directions as you travel. (Devices based on Google's Android operating system usually include live, turn-by-turn directions for free.) On the iPad 2, you must purchase an app from a provider such as Garmin, TomTom, Navigon, MotionX, or others to get live, turn-by-turn directions. These apps work best on a 3G iPad 2.

When traveling abroad, you may not have use of the 3G capability. Because of this, it may not be worth securing a data plan for your iPad 2 for just a few days in a given country. You still have use of the GPS hardware on your iPad, but you may not have a data connection to download maps when you're out of range of a Wi-Fi network.

NOTE: **Find My iPhone Works Better with 3G**

Apple's Find My iPhone app works for the iPad 2 as well as iPhones, but it requires two things: that you do the setup steps described in Lesson 5, and that your misplaced or stolen iPad 2 is accessible online. For a 3G-enabled iPad 2, this is usually possible because cell phone networks are so ubiquitous. For a Wi-Fi-only iPad 2, though, the device has to be connected to a nearby Wi-Fi network or it won't be accessible by the Find My iPhone app.

Using a WiFi-Only iPad 2

On a Wi-Fi-only iPad 2, or a 3G iPad 2 with no active 3G service, the picture is more complicated, but it does have some bright spots:

- **No true GPS location support**—The Wi-Fi-only iPad 2 units have no hardware GPS location support at all and can't use cell towers for location either. Your only location information support is from Wi-Fi networks whose digital signatures and physical locations are in a database from a company called Skyhook. Your location is triangulated from the nearest Wi-Fi base stations.

  If there's only one nearby Wi-Fi base station, and it covers a broad area, your location might be quite approximate. (This is shown by a big blue circle of uncertainty around the location marker in Maps.) If no Wi-Fi base stations are nearby, or if you're in a country with no Skyhook-type database, you can't get a location fix.

- **Limited data connection for maps**—With a Wi-Fi-only iPad 2, you won't usually have a Wi-Fi connection for updated map data when you're on the move, which is where you need it. If you have a map onscreen in Maps when you set out, it works until you leave that map, but you won't be able to get fresh map data.

- **Directions and saved maps**—You can get directions before you set out on your journey. You can also capture relevant map screens to the Photos app: get the map you want onscreen; then press the Home button and the Sleep/Wake switch simultaneously to capture the map into the Photos app. This is a poor substitute for true mapping support, but can be a very good substitute for paper maps.

  If you buy an app from a provider such as Garmin, TomTom, Navigon, or others, mapping information is included; you're limited only by the ability to get an accurate location using nearby Wi-Fi base stations.

▶ **Disappearing location support**—Location support from Wi-Fi base stations works quite well in most metropolitan areas with lots of Wi-Fi networks but disappears quite suddenly at many locations outside town. Don't expect to have solid location support with Wi-Fi as you would with a 3G unit with a more reliable data connection (for downloading maps) and better location support (for downloading the right map and showing where you are).

▶ **Tethering support**—You can tether your Wi-Fi-only iPad 2 to a smartphone, as described in Lesson 1. If you do this, you get the best of all worlds: true GPS support passed through from your smartphone, a robust data connection from your smartphone to get maps, and all the mapping capabilities of your iPad 2. The only worry is the high load placed on your smartphone's battery by supporting both tethering and GPS at the same time.

TIP: **With Wi-Fi, Preload Maps Before You Go**
Here's a trick that Wi-Fi users should be very aware of and that's also helpful for 3G users, if you go somewhere where you might not have a data connection: Map your route before you go. Zoom in at both ends of the journey before you leave, and get directions. Save the maps by pressing the Home button and the Sleep/Wake button at the same time; the image will be copied into the Photos app. You won't have "live" data for your current location, which is a big negative, but a preloaded map of this sort can at least take the place of a paper map.

▶ Traffic information on digital maps is spotty; and many of the things you really want to know—such as how long a traffic jam will last—can't be answered by a computer.

Benefits of Mapping on the iPad 2

There are many great things about using the iPad 2 for mapping. Let's look at some of the benefits:

▶ **It's functional when on the move**—There's a lot of functionality for free with a live Internet connection. Finding your location, getting directions, and adding support for geographically aware social networking are all at your fingertips.

▶ **It's functional at a Wi-Fi hotspot**—There's still a lot you can do when you're not on the move if you have a live Internet connection. You can look at maps, use Street View, get directions and save them for later use, and get local business information.

▶ **It's easy to use**—The size and direct tactile input of the iPad 2 are very well suited for use with online mapping, and the maps displayed look spectacular.

Follow the instructions in this lesson to get the most out of your mapping experience on iPad 2.

PLAIN ENGLISH: **Location Services**

Location services refers to all the capabilities your iPad 2 can bring to bear to help your iPad 2 identify its location. For a Wi-Fi-only iPad 2, this means using Wi-Fi base station locations—and, if you tether to a smartphone, the GPS on the smartphone. For a 3G iPad 2, location services also include GPS satellites and cell phone towers. In addition to Maps, which is offered standard on every iPad 2, other apps use location services. For instance, the Photos app uses location services to geo-tag photos whenever possible. For another example, if you purchase a mapping app with turn-by-turn navigation, it will use location services. (This kind of app might be frustratingly inaccurate with a Wi-Fi-only iPad 2.)

Searching for and Viewing Locations

Mapping is all about locations, of course. You can use your iPad 2 to search for locations, mark them, and view them in several modes, including in Street View.

Finding Your Current Location and Showing the Compass

For mapping and directions, it's very important to see where you are—or at least where the Maps app thinks you are! Follow these instructions to find yourself on the map:

1. Tap the Maps app to open and start it.

2. Tap the compass icon in the Maps app's status bar at the top of the screen. This re-centers the map on your current location, which is shown by a blue dot.

3. To get information about your current location, tap the blue dot. A brief description of your current location appears.

4. To see a fuller description of your current location, press the "i" in the brief description. A fuller description of your current location displays, with options, as shown in Figure 11.1. These options are described in the section "Finding Directions and Businesses."

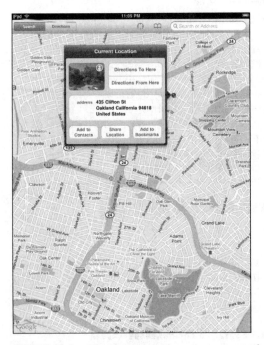

FIGURE 11.1 The Maps app gives you many options for each location.

5. To see your current location in Street View, press the Street View icon. Your location appears.

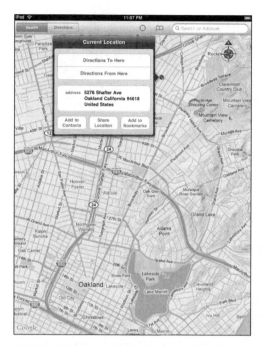

FIGURE 11.2   Let Google Maps on iPad 2 be your compass.

6. To show a digital compass, press the compass icon again. The map updates to show a compass icon and the direction of North, as shown in Figure 11.2 (shown in Terrain view, described later in this lesson). Hold the iPad 2 flat to see which way the compass is facing and find North. Text labels appear sideways unless you point the iPad 2 in a northerly direction.

7. To return to map view, without the compass, press the compass icon again.

CAUTION: **Turn Off GPS When You Can**

The GPS radio in the iPad 2 3G runs down your batteries, so turn it off when possible. You want to have it on, though, when using the Maps app or geo-aware apps and websites. The same thing is true with the GPS functionality on your smartphone, if your iPad 2 is tethered to it. An app or website will not necessarily tell you to turn on your system's GPS radio to provide information—it will simply provide geo-aware services if location information is available, and not provide them (or not provide them very well) if it isn't.

Therefore, it's up to you to figure out when you need GPS turned on (for more functionality) or off (to save power).

Using Street View

Street View is an amazing capability of the Maps app. Using Street View, you can navigate onscreen as if you were live and in person in places all over the world.

Google, which provides the Maps app and the data behind it, sent specially equipped cars and trucks around the streets and highways of most countries in the world to capture images, and then stitched them together to create panoramas of large areas, as seen from the road.

NOTE: **Use Street View for a Preview**

Street View can be a wonderful tool to help orient yourself to a destination you're traveling to. "Experiencing" the destination in Street View gives you a helpful tour of a new area, making it easier to find your way around when you get there.

The only thing more amazing than Street View itself is Street View as seen and used on the iPad 2. The large and bright screen, the fact that the iPad 2 is handheld, the way in which you can take it with you to get directions, and the way you manipulate the screen directly with your hands bring Street View to a new level.

Follow these steps to use Street View:

1. Bring up a description of a location, as described in the previous section.

2. Press the Street View icon to see the location in Street View.

   The location appears in Street View, as shown in Figure 11.3.

FIGURE 11.3   Street View immerses you in an onscreen "real world."

3. From Street View, use gestures to look around within the view. Drag the image to pan in all directions.

4. To change your location within Street View, press the arrows located on the road (where available). Your viewpoint will move down the road a little way in the indicated direction. You can then pan in all directions again. (Each such "jump" does not take you very far, so to move farther, you may want to zoom out, pan closer to your destination, and then return to Street View.)

5. To exit Street View, press the Map icon in the lower-right corner.

Using Map Views and Traffic

Google Maps defaults to what's called the Classic view. This is a map view with lots of useful detail, such as lot outlines for homes, businesses, and so on, for many locations.

To see additional views, put your finger in the lower-right corner, where it appears as if the map is curled away from the corner. Drag the corner up and to the left. You'll uncover mapping options, as shown in Figure 11.4.

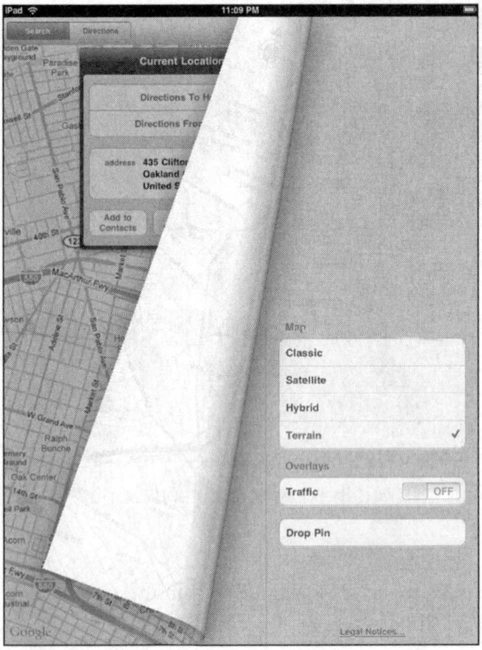

FIGURE 11.4   Mapping options give you lots of power.

Not all options are available for all locations. Where available, the mapping options are as follows:

- ▶ **Classic**—The default view that shows lot outlines, businesses, and other useful features.

- ▶ **Satellite**—A view made up of satellite photographs taken during the daytime on clear days. Shows an amazing level of detail.

- ▶ **Hybrid**—A very useful view for familiarizing yourself with an area (or just for gawking around in the area near your home, work, school, and so on). The Hybrid view combines text showing street names and business names, icons for things like transit stops, and satellite photography.

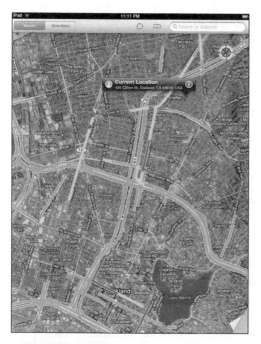

FIGURE 11.5   Traffic information can overlay any view, including the Satellite view.

▶ **Terrain**—A map showing elevations, street names, and major feature names, such as parks and university campuses. Great for planning a walk, a bicycle ride, or a hike.

▶ **Traffic**—An overlay that shows traffic conditions on major streets, highways, and freeways, shown overlaying the Terrain map on Figure 11.5. Green shows roads operating at or near top posted speed—or, for highways and freeways, more than 50 mph; yellow is slower than the posted speed—or, for highways and freeways, from 25–50 mph; and red is below 25 mph.

▶ **Drop pin**—Puts a pin into the map that you can use to get information on that location. You can also drop a pin by pressing and holding on the map directly.

Finding Destinations and Businesses

Finding locations is easy on iPad 2, although entering addresses using the onscreen keyboard can be a bit tricky. This is especially true because you may find yourself switching among the alphabetic, numeric, and special characters versions of the onscreen keyboard a lot to enter an address. It might take you a couple of tries to get the address right.

After you find a location, you can view it (including in Street View, where available) and drop a pin on locations of your own.

Follow these steps to search for a location:

1. Press the Search button in the upper-left corner. The map you've viewed most recently in Search appears.

2. Press the Search field. Press the X to clear it, if needed. The onscreen keyboard appears, along with a list of recent searches.

3. Type an address or other search information. Google is pretty good with relatively free-form searches, but the most reliable format is still the street address (number and street name) followed by the city name, or an abbreviation for the city name ("sf" or "nyc", for instance).

You can also try more general searches, such as "picante berk" for a Mexican food restaurant in Berkeley, California, but be careful of multiple matches and mismatches. You might end up being steered to the Berkshires in Massachusetts!

4. Press Search on the keyboard.

One or more pins appear to show matches for your search.

5. Use gestures such as pinching to zoom and panning to look at different areas of the map to focus in on the pin(s). If there are multiple pins, tap a pin to see the descriptor for it.

The destination becomes a Recent, meaning it appears in the Recents list for searches and for creating directions.

6. Tap the blue "i" on a descriptor to see detailed information about a location.

Detailed information about the location appears, as described earlier in this lesson.

7. Press one of the buttons in the information to get directions to the destination or directions from the destination to somewhere else, to add the destination to your Contacts, to share the destination via email (this doesn't close the Maps app), or to add the location to your Bookmarks. Press the URL, if one is provided, to go to the associated web page (this does close the Maps app). Press the Street View icon to see the location in Street View, as described earlier in this lesson.

NOTE: **Directions and Bookmarks**

For information about getting directions, or about using Maps Bookmarks, see the relevant sections later in this lesson.

Sharing the destination via email gives you a chance to add a note, and then send both a Microsoft Outlook business card file and a Google Maps link to the destination.

8. To drop a pin on a location, zoom in very tightly (down to the level where you can see lot lines, where available); then press on the map in the desired spot. A pin appears, showing the destination address.

9. To see and use options for the dropped pin's location, press the blue "i" button. Options appear, as shown previously in Figure 11.4 and described in step 7.

10. To remove the pin, press the Remove Pin button in the information area.

CAUTION: **Watch Out for "Big" Destinations**

It's easy to get "bad" locations and directions for some destinations. Many hospitals and restaurants, among others, have several locations. Universities, national parks, and other geographically extensive destinations often have multiple entrances or addresses, some of which may be miles from where you actually want to go, such as the entrance to a national park or the main parking lot. Double-check that you're being pointed to the right destination; you may need to check a website or call ahead to be sure.

NOTE: **Directions—Yes, Turn-by-Turn—No**
The Maps app does a great many useful things, including provide directions for your journey. It does not, though, provide live, step-by-step, turn-by-turn directions during your trip. Neither the iPhone nor the iPad product families provide this service, whereas devices based on the Android operating system generally do. If you want this capability on an iOS device, you need a specialized app for it, and you want a 3G iPad, with its built-in GPS hardware, for best results. Check in the App Store, described in Lesson 12, for details.

Getting Directions and Using Bookmarks

Getting directions, and helping you follow them, is one of the most useful things a portable device can do. With iPad 2, directions are uniquely functional because of the size of the display and the way you manipulate the screen directly.

Follow these steps to view directions:

1. To make entering directions easier, first find the start and end points onscreen (if neither of them is your current location or already a Recent), as described in the previous section. The start or end point will now appear in the Recents list for searches, making it easy to select that point for directions.

2. To make a point a Bookmark, touch its pin to open the information area for it, as described in the previous section. Press Add to Bookmarks; the Add Bookmark window opens. Edit the name, using the onscreen keyboard, and press Save.

3. To begin getting directions, press the Directions button in the upper right. Or, from a location description or a Bookmark (press

the Bookmarks icon), press the Directions to Here button or the Directions from Here button. The Start-End area appears in the upper-right corner of the screen. The Start and/or End areas may be filled in with Current Location or a spot that you specified.

4. To enter or change the Start location, press in the first area. A list of Recents appears, and the onscreen keyboard appears as well, as shown in Figure 11.6.

FIGURE 11.6   Recents and Bookmarks help you generate directions quickly and easily.

5. Press a Recent to choose it, or enter an address using the onscreen keyboard, as described in the previous section.

6. Enter the End location—press in the Destination area to search, use a Recent, or use a Bookmark, as described in the previous steps. The End location appears onscreen, as does a strip to select Driving, Transit, or Walking directions.

7. Choose Driving, Transit, or Walking. For Transit, press the Time button and then press Depart to enter the time of departure or arrival, as shown in Figure 11.7.

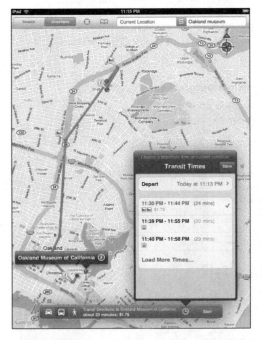

FIGURE 11.7   You can select Driving, Transit (with times), or Walking directions. You can view estimated travel time, distance, and/or cost for the directions you choose.

8. Press Start to view the directions. The directions appear in the strip at the bottom of the screen.

9. To see step-by-step directions, press the arrow keys at the bottom of the screen. To see complete directions, press the list icon; the list of steps appears onscreen, as shown in Figure 11.8.

To get the most useful information onscreen at once, you can pinch to zoom and drag the map "underneath" the list, or turn the iPad 2 to portrait or landscape mode, without disturbing the directions list or changing its relative location.

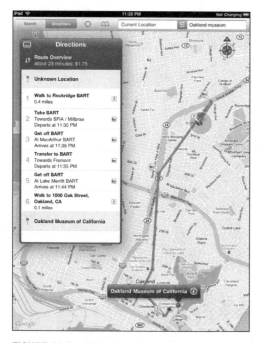

FIGURE 11.8 This directions list shows walking, Bay Area Rapid Transit (BART) stops, and costs.

Summary

In this lesson, you learned what to expect from the location services and Maps app for either a Wi-Fi-only iPad 2 or a 3G unit. You also learned how to use the Maps app to find your current location, get directions, use Street View and other views, get traffic updates, and more. In the next lesson, I show you how to get the most out of the App Store by getting apps for your iPad 2.

LESSON 12

Getting Apps from the App Store

In this lesson, you learn about apps: how to find, purchase (if necessary), and download them from the App Store on iPad 2. You also learn how to rate, report problems with, and update apps.

Understanding the App Store's Success

The Apple App Store for the iPod Touch, iPhone, and now the iPad and iPad 2 is an amazing success story, and one of the most important reasons that the iPad and iPad 2 have gotten off to such a great start as new products.

The original idea for the iPhone was that the only add-on software for it would be in the form of custom web pages written in the still-emerging technology, HTML5. The custom web page would be loaded automatically whenever an iPhone visited the website. This is good to understand, because web pages are still an important tool for delivering software functionality on all iOS devices, including the iPad 2, today.

The App Store was developed because developers asked Apple for a way to create apps like the ones that Apple put on the iPod and iPhone—Mail, Maps, and so on. Apple obliged, and the App Store has become an unexpected hit.

Aside from the size of its screen, the iPad 2 is not much different from the iPhone. However, the iPad 2's larger screen is an important difference because, with five times more space, more relevant information is available onscreen at once, making many tasks easier to complete. Also, the iPad 2 inherits the App Store infrastructure, while adding just a bit of complexity to it.

There are now three major kinds of apps, as follows:

▶ **iPad-specific apps**—One bundle of software that works only on iPad and iPad 2.

▶ **Universal apps**—A bundle of software with an extra chunk of software code and two sets of graphics: one for the iPad and iPad 2 and one for iPhones. The app runs in the appropriate resolution on either platform.

▶ **iPhone-specific apps**—These apps are made to run on iPhone only, and have iPhone-sized graphics.

There's no real problem with using iPhone-specific apps on the iPad or iPad 2. You download and run them just like a universal app or an iPad-specific app. The only difference is that when you run an iPhone-specific app on the iPad 2, it appears small compared to iPad apps, albeit very crisp looking.

If you want, you can expand the app to nearly full screen by pushing the 2x button that appears onscreen when you run an iPhone app on an iPad 2. Pushing this button makes the app display in a bigger size, and makes it easier to touch the right spots on the app to control it. However, using the 2x button, known as "screen doubling," makes the graphics look a bit rough and unfinished, as shown in Figure 12.1. To return to small-but-crisp mode, push the 1x button, and the image shrinks down again.

You'll want to run iPad-specific or universal apps when you can, to get the full use of the power of the iPad 2's far-larger screen. As the iPad and iPad 2 user base grows, more iPhone apps will likely be upgraded to support iPad and iPad 2 as well, either in an iPad-specific version or as a universal app.

CAUTION: **Stick with the App Store**

For most iPhone and iPad 2 users, the only way to get apps is through Apple's App Store. Some users "jailbreak" their devices,

---

allowing them to run non-App Store apps. However, if you do this, you violate your device's warranty, risk loss of access to the App Store, and open yourself up to potential problems, such as viruses and fraud.

FIGURE 12.1   iPhone-specific apps work fine on iPad 2.

TIP: **Apps Help with Flash**

Although more and more websites provide non-Flash versions of content for use by Apple-made iOS devices, there are still a lot of sites that use Flash. You can get apps that help you use Flash content embedded in web pages on your iPad 2. The translation of Flash into an iPad-friendly format can take place on the app maker's servers or on your iPad 2. Each approach has its own advantages and disadvantages. Two apps worth looking into that translate Flash content are Swifter and Skyfire, but new apps appear constantly, and existing ones are frequently updated. Check the App Store for the latest and greatest if you need access to Flash content through your iPad 2.

Finding Out About Apps

Apple has made famous the line, "There's an app for that," to describe just how much apps can do for you. There are roughly 350,000 apps in Apple's App Store at this writing, with about 65,000 of them being iPad-specific. A few apps, especially games, are specific to the iPad 2, or work better on the iPad 2, because they take advantage of the iPad 2's 3-axis gyroscope or built-in cameras.

With so many apps, it's impossible for any user to research all of them, or even to carefully look into all the apps in a given category. Instead, people use several techniques to find apps, as follows:

▶ Reading ads, from Apple and others, that highlight apps

▶ Reading the press, including the specialized technology press

▶ Talking to friends, family members, and business colleagues

▶ Searching in the App Store through iTunes or on your iPad 2

▶ Broad searches on the web (not in the App Store)

I recommend that you use several, if not all, of these techniques in combination. By taking this approach, you get the "official" information and user reviews in the App Store, plus a wide range of other information and opinions from your broader search, all of which are needed to help you make good decisions on how to use your precious time, money (for apps that aren't free), and attention.

Apple has a website for iPad apps, including iPad 2-specific apps, at http://www.apple.com/ipad/from-the-app-store/, shown in Figure 12.2. Use this site to research and learn about some of the top apps for iPad. You can also use sites like Gizmodo, TechCrunch, Mashable, and many others. (It may prove to be helpful to search on an app name to find sites that have written about the app, and then search the sites you find in more depth to see what other iPad 2 apps they recommend.)

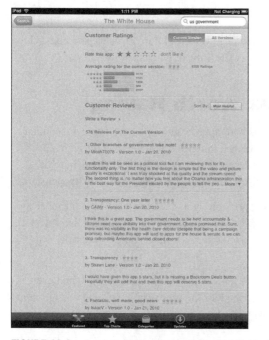

FIGURE 12.2   Apple's iPad apps website highlights top offerings.

One topic of particular interest is money. In many cases, you can get free apps that do at least the core things that a paid-for app does. Some apps have a higher-priced version, and also a lower-priced or free version, often including advertising or reduced functionality. You can try the free or less expensive version, then upgrade if you need more functionality. You may also find a website that you can visit for free from your iPad 2 that does much or all of what an app does.

> TIP: **Use a Computer First**
> Do broad searches for information about apps on your personal computer, which gives you more screen space than the iPad 2 and

> the ability to more easily move among multiple browser windows, and then search in the App Store for the specific app.

Use your research to find free or lower-cost alternatives to paid apps. One site that highlights free apps is iPadLuv, at www.ipadluv.net.

Finding Apps Worth Having

One of the biggest problems with apps is an ironic one: There are so many apps out there that finding the one you need may be quite difficult. Also, there can be an app that does something you really want done, but you don't realize that it's even available until you hear about it by happenstance.

To get the most out of the App Store, you need to spend time meandering through it. Look at some of the apps on display in categories that interest you to get an idea of what's available, as well as some inspiration as to what you might need.

The apps in the App Store are constantly changing; new apps, and even new types of apps, are introduced all the time. The long-time champion in a category can suddenly be upset by a newcomer or an improved version of a competing app.

With that caveat in mind, I've created a short list of some very hot iPad apps that are particularly useful on the iPad 2, or simply indispensable on any iPad, or both. Prices tend to change with time, so I've listed the apps as either free or paid; the paid apps are almost all $5 or less. You might get some good ideas from this list of popular apps used on the iPad 2, in various categories:

- ▶ **File storage**—Dropbox (free) is a popular service for storing files "in the cloud," to be accessed from any connected device: personal computer, smartphone, iPad 2, and so on.

- ▶ **Games**—At this writing, games that take full advantage of the iPad 2—its 3-axis gyroscope, fast processing speed, and fast graphics—are still under development. Infinity Blade (paid) is a game written for the original iPad, before the iPad 2 came out; however, it uses rendered 3D graphics that look noticeably better on the iPad 2 than on the iPad.

▶ **Lost iPad**—Apple has a free service, Find My iPhone, that works for the iPad too. Enable it in Settings, as described in Lesson 5. Then, if you lose your phone, you can sign into the Apple website at www.apple.com, or use the Find My iPhone app on any iOS device to track it down. (You can download the app when you need it and try to access your iPad 2, as long as you completed the setup steps described in Lesson 5.)

▶ **Fixing photos**—You may not believe it until you see it, but Adobe's Photoshop Express is an iPad app; so are cool, innovative apps like Photogene, FilterStorm, and PictureShow. These work on the low-res photos you can capture with the iPad 2's cameras as well as higher-resolution images from better cameras. These apps make a virtue of the touch interface to make you more effective with photos. Shop carefully—photo apps are relatively expensive, though the best of them are well worth the money.

▶ **Making movies**—Apple's iMovie software (paid) has long helped Mac users get the most out of their camcorders, smartphones with video capability, and other video sources. With the launch of iPad 2, Apple launched iMovie for iPad, which takes advantage of the iPad 2's cameras as well as its fast processing speed and additional RAM to make movie editing practical on a tablet device.

▶ **Making music**—There are many creative apps for making music with your iPad 2, and they all benefit from the speed and easy mobility of the device. (However, don't play air guitar with your iPad 2 in hand too energetically, or you might drop it.) With the launch of the iPad 2, Apple introduced GarageBand (paid— shown in Figure 12.3), which combines external sounds, digital instruments, and an 8-track recording studio—all so easy to use that even beginners can make interesting sounds.

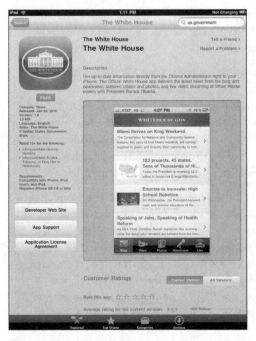

FIGURE 12.3   GarageBand helps you rock the house.

▶ **Offline access**—Instapaper (free and paid) allows you to mark a web page for storage from a browser running on any device. You sync Instapaper from your iPad 2 when you have an online connection, and the web page is then available on your iPad 2 even when you're not connected. Great for users of Wi-Fi-only iPads who need to get through their online reading, but can't always be online.

▶ **Online reading**—Flipboard (paid) is a social magazine; it brings in content from Twitter, Facebook, and RSS feeds, and then lays it out in an attractive, easy-to-read format. Flipboard works even better on the iPad 2 because of the device's speed.

▶ **Printing**—There are many inexpensive apps that help you print from your iPad 2 to just about any printer. AirPrint Activator (free) helps you print from the iPad 2 to a shared printer.

▶ **Radio**—If you can't live without your radio, TuneInRadio (paid) is an app that will turn your iPad 2 into one. It allows you to listen to online radio stations freely and flexibly. You can set an alarm to wake up to your favorite station. There are also many streaming music apps, of which the best known is Pandora.

▶ **Social networks**—Excellent official and unofficial iPad apps exist for just about any social networking tool out there, including Twitter and Foursquare. The big exception is Facebook, which—at least up to this writing—considers iPad 2 to be non-mobile; use touch.facebook.com in your browser instead. Or fire up the leading unofficial Facebook app, Friendly.

Finding and Downloading Apps

There are two ways to get apps onto your iPad 2. One approach is to search in Apple's App Store using iTunes, and then download the app to iTunes. The next time you synchronize your iPad 2 with your personal computer, the app is transferred to your iPad 2. Apps you purchase for your iPod Touch or iPhone will also be automatically synchronized to your iPad 2, and will work fine there.

However, many iPad 2 users, including me, like to do as much directly on the iPad 2 as reasonably possible. So, another approach is to find and download apps directly onto your iPad 2. This way, there's no waiting for your iPad 2 to sync in order to use your app. The app will be backed up into iTunes on your personal computer the next time you sync.

To purchase apps or iTunes content, you need an iTunes account linked to a credit card or iTunes gift card. You will be asked to provide the relevant information if you try to download an app or paid content without having provided payment information. For instructions about using iTunes to sync any existing apps you already have onto your iPad 2, see Lesson 18, "Using iTunes and Home Sharing."

NOTE: **Get an iTunes Account**

You must have an iTunes store account with payment information to download applications, even free ones. Go to Settings, Store to set

up a new account and add payment information if needed. See
Lesson 18 for details.

Follow these steps to find apps in the App Store:

1. Tap the App Store app to start it.

2. Tap either the Featured, Top Charts, or Categories icon at the bottom of the screen to look for apps that interest you and fit your needs.

You can find various special designations like the App of the Week, Staff Favorites, and others. iPad-specific apps, which are the more desirable choice in most cases, are sometimes designated HD (for High Definition) or XL (for eXtra Large, referring to the iPad's larger screen), or have iPad in the name ("Twitterific for iPad" is an example). However, there is not always a specific iPad designation for an iPad app.

NOTE: **Redeem Your Codes**

If you have a redemption code for an app—for instance, one obtained from the developer's website—use the Redeem button at the bottom of the Featured screen or the Top Charts screen, then enter the code.

3. Search using keywords to find apps of interest, or to find specific apps that you have learned about through research on your personal computer and elsewhere.

4. When you see an app you like on a page or in a list of search results, tap the brief description to see more. A full description appears on the Info screen, as shown in Figure 12.4.

5. To see customer ratings and reviews, scroll down. To see screenshots (where available), scroll down and then flick through screenshots. To see additional apps from the same developer (where available), scroll down and then look in the left column.

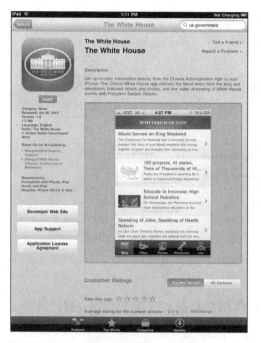

FIGURE 12.4   App descriptions entice you to add even more apps.

NOTE: **Use Ratings First**

The ratings and comments are quite helpful in understanding the strong and weak points of an app, including the specifics of how well it looks and works on iPad, in contrast to iPhone or other platforms it might run on.

---

6. To install the app on your iPad 2, press the button in the upper-left corner, which either says Free or has the app's price on it.

7. Enter your iTunes password.

   The app starts downloading. You're taken to a page on your iPad 2's Home screen where the app icon appears, and you can watch the icon fill in as the app downloads.

8. To use the app after it downloads, tap its icon.

NOTE: **App Downloads Recover**

If an app download is interrupted by a lost connection or a server problem, it resumes the next time you connect. Alternatively, you can open iTunes on your personal computer, and the app downloads to iTunes, and then is copied to your iPad 2 the next time you sync.

CAUTION: **No Deposit, No Return**

At this writing, the App Store's return policy is: There are no returns, except if the App Store fails to deliver the app to you within a reasonable period of time. There is no trial period for apps you purchase. So, research apps carefully—including, if possible, trying the app out on the iPad or iPad 2 of a friend who's already purchased it—before buying.

Following Up After Installing an App

After you download an app and install it, you may need technical support, want to write a review, or want to share your opinion of the app with friends. The App Store supports all these needs:

- ▶ **Rating apps**—Ratings are a big help in choosing which apps to use. To rate the app, press the appropriate number of stars on the app's Info page and then enter any comments. See Figure 12.5 for examples of ratings for an app.

- ▶ **Reporting problems**—To report a problem with the app, press the Report a Problem link at the upper right of the screen. For app support, press the App Support button. (The difference between Report a Problem and App Support is not always clear, and varies from app to app.)

- ▶ **Updating applications**—The App Store icon displays a number on the icon to show any application updates that are available. To install the update(s), open the App Store and press the Updates icon at the bottom of the screen. Then press the icon for each app

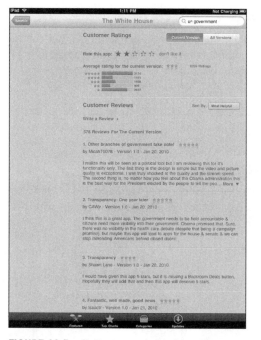

FIGURE 12.5 Rating apps is kind to others.

that needs an update, or press the Update All Apps button; the update will install.

▶ **Uninstalling**—To uninstall an app, press and hold the app's icon until it wiggles onscreen; then tap the X that appears next to the icon. The app disappears from the screen, and its data is no longer accessible, but it isn't erased from iPad 2.

▶ **Clearing settings and data**—If you want, you can uninstall an app, and then "buy" it again in the App Store. (You shouldn't be charged again for the repeat "purchase" of a paid-for app.) Uninstalling and restoring has the effect of restoring the app to its default settings, minus any settings you've changed and data you've entered into the app. This is a commonly recommended way of solving problems with an app.

> TIP: **App Store Keeps Track**
>
> The App Store keeps track of which apps you install and/or buy. Any apps you download and install onto your iPad 2 are copied into iTunes the next time you sync. So, there's no risk of losing track of an app once you download it, or of losing money you've spent on an app purchase.

Summary

In this lesson, you learned how to find out about apps, download and install them, and follow up by rating apps, reporting on problems, and updating them. In the next lesson, I show you how to take photos with your iPad 2 and edit them.

LESSON 13

Taking Photos

In this lesson, you learn about the strengths and weaknesses of the iPad 2's front- and rear-facing cameras. You then learn how to use the cameras to take photos and capture movie clips.

Knowing When to Use the iPad's Camera

Including cameras in the iPad 2 is a breakthrough, enabling all sorts of cool things to happen. However, these cameras are very low-resolution devices. A typical smartphone camera today has a resolution of 5Mpx—that's 5 million pixels—or more. A 2Mpx resolution is the least you'd want to use for a photo that you were thinking of printing. But the cameras on the iPad 2 have a resolution of 0.3Mpx, for the front-facing camera, and 0.7Mpx for the rear-facing one.

As the Ross character on the TV show *Friends* once said, "Why? Why? Why? Why?" The reason is simple. The cameras are there for video phone calls, not for taking still photos. Low-resolution cameras make it practical to send a stream of images over the Internet smoothly. Even with a Wi-Fi connection, you don't want to put high-resolution images at 30 frames per second over the Internet, or you'll have problems.

The front-facing camera has to deliver a rock-steady image of your beautiful face, with no missed frames—which means no skips, jumps, or artifacts. So, having it be a mere 640×480 in resolution—even less than the iPad's screen—makes sense. The small images, 0.3Mpx each, still require a healthy 10Mbps of bandwidth to transmit adequately.

Figure 13.1 shows images taken with the front-facing and rear-facing cameras on the iPad 2. A figure printed in a book can give you only a rough idea of what an actual photo taken with the iPad 2 looks like, so plan to do some experimentation to develop your own idea as to the quality of photos from the iPad 2.

FIGURE 13.1 Photos taken with the iPad 2's front-facing camera (top) and rear-facing camera (bottom).

TIP: **"Taking a Picture" During a Video Phone Call**

If you want to capture what's going on during a video phone call, you can do a screen grab of everything that's onscreen at the time, including your own beautiful face. Just press the Home button and the Sleep/Wake switch simultaneously, and the iPad will capture the current screen image and store it in the Photos app.

The rear-facing camera is likely to be used for a live sweep across a panoramic scene or a group of friends, to illustrate where you are or who you're with, or to take short movie clips. In this mode, the rear-facing camera uses 720p resolution, which is 1280×720 pixels.

Apple also knew that the rear-facing camera would be used for pictures some of the time. So, they picked the lowest-resolution camera they could that would be just good enough for the occasional picture, but with image sizes small enough to not completely swamp your Internet connection. The 0.7Mpx rear-facing camera fits the bill.

The image size for stills is 960×720 pixels, a little smaller than the full iPad 2 screen. The reason the still image resolution is less than the video resolution is that the edges of the image are cut off to make the photo more square.

Cost issues may have had an impact, too. For instance, the lowest-end iPad 2, the $499 Wi-Fi-only iPad 2 with 16GB of flash memory, is surprisingly affordable; so much so that competitors have had a very hard time producing a comparable unit for the same price. Using low-resolution cameras no doubt helps keep Apple's costs down, so they can meet aggressive price points.

There are other reasons not to use the iPad 2's rear-facing camera for photos very often. The low resolution means that images have to be well lit to look decent. There's no flash on the iPad 2, so the need for good existing light is increased further. And using the iPad 2 as a camera is physically tricky; the iPad 2 is quite compact for a tablet computer, but it's bulky and clumsy indeed for a camera. Also, consider that even if you only have your mobile phone with you, you probably have a much better camera on hand. And an actual digital camera is likely to give you even better results.

With all that, it's still tempting to use the iPad 2 camera fairly often. Photographers say that "the best camera is the one you have with you when you need it," so if you have the iPad 2 with you, you likely want to use the camera. Because it takes time and effort to transfer pictures from another device to the iPad 2, taking the picture with the iPad 2 seems easier. And it's kind of fun to take photos with a viewfinder nearly the size of a sheet of letter paper.

It's worth mentioning that all of the same applies to movie clips. Apple makes the iMovie iPad app available for just $4.99, and it's very fun and easy to use. Also, the poor resolution of the iPad's cameras isn't quite as much of a problem with movies, because the scene is more likely to change as people, and you, move about. This makes problems with the individual images that make up the movie clip much less noticeable.

So, it seems tempting to simply snap a picture, or make a movie clip, with your iPad 2 and start editing it. The trouble with this is, when you take a picture or capture a movie clip with the iPad 2 and then start editing it, you spend your precious time working on low-quality images.

Wait, it gets worse: There are no controls for the image you capture with your iPad 2. No zooming in and out, no light balance adjustments, nothing. Again, a typical mobile phone camera or a true digital camera is a much better bet for anything except the most spontaneous photos or movie clips.

However, here are two suggestions for getting the best results for photos with your iPad 2:

Learn how to transfer photos and movie clips from your smartphone and/or digital camera to the iPad 2. (From a smartphone, you can usually transfer a single image easily by sending it as an email attachment.) If you master the technique of transferring images, doing it becomes less of a barrier, and then you have more high-quality images to work with on your iPad 2.

Only take photos with the iPad 2 itself if you just need a quickly captured image to attach to an email or for a similar use. Some examples are a quick picture for Facebook of who you're with or where you are; emailing a photo of a menu to someone (however, small text may be illegible); or giving a friend an idea of the length of the line to, say, buy a new iPad 2.

You can often improve photos with a third-party editing tool such as PhotoShop Express. You can get rid of red eye, bring out details, and so on. However, one of the hardest problems to fix is a photo that lacks enough resolution in the first place. So, if the picture is important, use a better camera if you can—and use the iPad 2's camera, plus a tool like Photoshop Express, if you have to.

You can be a little more lenient on yourself with movie clips, because the resolution situation is better. Still, you may end up with regrets if the only recording you have of an important event is photos and/or movie clips from your iPad 2. Use a "real" still camera or video camera if at all possible.

Capturing a Photo or Movie Clip

Taking a photo or capturing a movie clip with the iPad 2 is easy:

1. Hold the iPad 2 in landscape mode, with the Home button to the right.

   Holding the iPad 2 this way puts the camera lens on the upper edge of the iPad 2, away from the lower edge—where your fingers are positioned to hold the device.

2. From the Home screen, press the icon for the Photo app.

   The Photo app opens, displaying the live image from the front or rear camera, as shown in Figure 13.2.

FIGURE 13.2   The live view from your iPad 2 is so big and lively, it's disconcerting at first.

3. If needed, press the Swap button to swap from the current camera—front-facing or rear-facing—to the other one. Drag the Camera/Movie slider to choose between still photos and video clips.

In most cases, you want to use the rear-facing camera, even for a picture of yourself. The resolution of the rear-facing camera, while poor, is more than twice as good as the resolution of the front-facing camera.

NOTE: **Using Photobooth**

Using Photobooth is fun. Just open Photobooth instead of the Camera app. Pick an effect from among the nine options, as shown in Figure 13.3, and then take your picture. It is captured just like a normal picture, but with the Photobooth effect added.

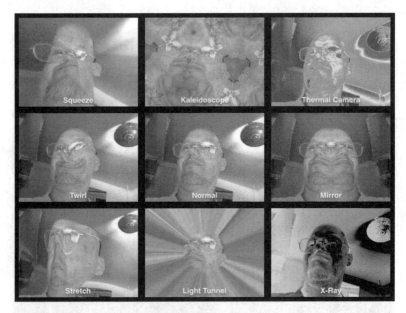

FIGURE 13.3 Choose an effect in Photobooth, and then take your picture.

4. To take a picture, drag the slider to the photo position, point the iPad 2 at the subject, move closer or farther to the subject (if possible) to zoom in or out, and then press the shutter button. To make a movie, skip to step 6.

The photo is captured, and a small thumbnail representing the image appears in the lower right of the screen.

5. To see the image you just captured in iPhoto, tap the thumbnail.

   The photo opens in iPhoto. For information about working with photos and movie clips, see Lesson 14.

6. To make a movie clip, drag the slider to the movie position, point the iPad 2 at the subject, move closer or farther to the subject (if possible) to zoom in or out, and then press the Record button.

   The iPad 2 starts recording.

7. To stop recording, press the Record button again.

   A small thumbnail appears in the lower left of the screen representing the image.

8. To see the movie clip you just captured in Photos, tap the thumbnail.

   The movie clip opens in Photos. For information about working with photos and movie clips in Photos, refer to Lesson 14.

Summary

In this lesson, you learned about the strengths and weaknesses of the iPad 2's front- and rear-facing cameras. You then learned how to use the cameras to take photos and capture movie clips. In the next lesson, you learn how to use Apple's Photos app.

LESSON 14

Importing and Viewing Photos

In this lesson, you learn how to import photos from the iPad 2's cameras and from your personal computer or a digital camera or cellphone; how to get photos through screenshots and downloading attachments; how to view photos onscreen, in albums, as wallpaper, and in the Picture Frame feature; and how to share photos.

Photos on the iPad 2

The iPad 2 might be the best device yet for storing, arranging, and sharing photos. It is both easier to use and more powerful than the old-fashioned photo album. The iPad 2 displays digital photographs in a nice, large size—much larger than viewing on a smartphone—beautifully backlit, and in full color. At the same time, the iPad 2's thinness, light weight, and flexibility make it easy to share photos with others.

Your iPad 2 supports a wide range of photo formats, including the following:

▶ **JPEG**—JPEG is short for Joint Photographic Experts Group, a carefully crafted standard for compressing photo files by 90% or more with little visible loss of quality. If you are saving photos in JPEG format for use on the iPad 2 from a graphics program such as Photoshop, consider using a resolution of about 150 dpi and roughly 80% compression.

CAUTION: **Don't Use JPEG Twice**

JPEG is great, but the common practice of compressing the same photo through JPEG three or four times amplifies the worst effects

> of JPEG compression, so don't run them through JPEG compression more than once.

> ▶ **TIFF**—TIFF means Tagged Image File Format. TIFF is a loss-less format, so photographs are big (in file size) and beautiful. When you get a JPEG file and edit it, consider saving the result as TIFF or PNG to avoid the degradation inherent in multiple JPEG compression cycles. (You may still need to save the final result as JPEG, in order to reduce the final file size.)

> ▶ **GIF**—GIF, or Graphics Image Format, has small file sizes but is limited to 256 colors. It is very hard on any but black-and-white images or the smallest photos. Avoid GIF for photos in most cases. It's suitable for many simpler (in terms of color usage) computer-generated images, though.

> ▶ **PNG**—PNG, originally defined as standing for "PNG's Not GIF," officially stands for Portable Network Graphics. PNG is much like GIF, but without the 256-color limitation. As a lossless format, without GIF's limitation to 256 colors, PNG is an increasingly popular file format for images of all sorts.

The iPad 2's role with photos highlights one of the criticisms of the original iPad: unlike a personal computer, it's used more for consuming media and information than for creating it. The original iPad doesn't have a camera in it. Photos have to be taken on other devices and imported into the iPad, definitely leading to delayed gratification.

Unfortunately, the iPad 2 doesn't entirely solve the problem. Neither the rear-facing camera, with its resolution of 0.7Mpx, nor the front-facing camera, with its mere 0.3Mpx resolution, takes photos good enough for display on an iPad, let alone for use on a bigger computer screen. And iPad 2 photos from either camera look really bad printed out.

The iPad 2 cameras are good for a quick "this is it" snapshot, but not for anything that needs to look good. Use other cameras and import the images to keep the photos in your Photos app up to snuff.

The iPad 2 also suffers as a photo manager in comparison to a personal computer. The iPad 2 resizes photos to fit the iPad 2 screen. The iPad 2 screen is big enough that the resulting resized image is fine for most digital uses. However, if you want to keep the original, higher-resolution file—and especially if you ever plan to print the image at a typical photo size, such as 4" x 6", or even larger—then don't use the iPad 2 as the only repository for your images.

In addition, there's a concern with storage space. Even a moderately compressed photo on the iPad 2 takes up about 1MB of space. That's 1,000 photos per gigabyte, which sounds like a lot, but adds up pretty fast. This is far less of a concern on a personal computer, with its hard disk that is many times larger than the static RAM that's used for long-term storage in an iPad 2.

The presence of cameras on an iPad 2 also makes it that much easier to overload your iPad 2 with pictures that really aren't worth keeping, or displaying. One of the coolest features of the iPad 2 is the slideshow or Picture Frame option, as described later in this lesson. But the slideshow is only as good as the quality of the photos in it. Be sure to aggressively prune photos on your iPad 2, so you keep only the best over the long haul. (You should also store higher-resolution versions of your favorite photos on your computer, where they keep their full resolution.)

If these concerns resonate for you, consider using your personal computer for your photo management tasks instead of the iPad 2; use the iPad 2 as a portable display device. Also, consider keeping a higher quality digital camera—potentially the one on your mobile phone—with you just about all the time, so you are less tempted to take photos with the iPad 2. The iPad 2 remains a great device for viewing and sharing photos. Use the information and steps in this lesson to help you get the most out of it.

> CAUTION: **iPad 2 Resizes Photos**
> When iPad 2 imports photos, it resizes them as necessary to fit its screen. This is fine for viewing photos on iPad 2. However, if keeping the original, highest-resolution version of the images is important to you, don't use iPad 2 as your only storage device.

Synchronizing Photos with Other Devices

The original iPod music player, used with iTunes software, depended on a personal computer as the organizing hub for music files. As the iPod line added movies, phone capabilities (the iPhone), and now the enhanced capabilities of the iPad 2, this personal computer-centric organizing principle has remained.

If you use a personal computer as a kind of media control panel, your life with your iPad 2 is easy. Just continue bringing photos to your personal computer from one or more devices, then sync your iPad 2 to your personal computer using iTunes. (Syncing using iTunes is described in Lesson 18, "Using iTunes and Home Sharing.")

You can also sync digital photos directly from a camera, cellphone, or SD memory card. To do this, you need the iPad Camera Connection Kit, described in Lesson 1, "Introducing iPad 2."

> NOTE: **USB Just for Cameras**
>
> The USB Camera Connector supports only cameras, not other USB devices.

Follow these steps to sync digital photos using the iPad Camera Connection Kit:

1. Insert the SD Card Reader or USB Camera Connector into the iPad 2 dock connector port.

2. For an SD memory card, insert it into the slot on the SD Card Reader. For a camera, iPhone, or other cell phone that takes pictures, use that device's USB cable to connect to the USB Camera Connector. Make sure the device is turned on and, if applicable, in transfer mode.

   For the SD memory card, insert the card gently, because it will fit only in one orientation. (For other devices, see the device's documentation for details.)

   Your iPad 2 automatically opens the Photos application and displays the photos that it can import from the device or SD card you've connected.

3. To import all the photos, tap Import All. To import specific photos, tap the photo's thumbnail image to place check marks next to the ones you want; then tap Import.

The photos are imported to your iPad 2, which may take a few seconds (see Figure 14.1).

FIGURE 14.1   Photos come to life on iPad 2.

4. Choose whether to keep or delete the photos on the device or SD card you've connected.

5. Disconnect the SD Card Reader or USB Camera Connector.

6. View the photos in the Last Import album in the Photos app.

7. Transfer the photos to your personal computer by connecting the iPad 2 to the personal computer using USB and importing the images with a photo program, such as Adobe Photoshop Elements or Apple's iPhoto.

TIP: **Get Rid of Extra Photos**

Consider developing a routine for transferring photos to your PC, which is great for storing high-resolution versions of photos. Transfer photos that you want to show off to people—or use with an iPad app—to your iPad 2, and possibly to other devices. Then delete the file from the original device at some point in the process, so the original device doesn't fill up with photo files.

Viewing Photos on the iPad 2

Viewing photos on iPad 2 is enjoyable. I've seen professional photographers buy several iPads and iPad 2s simply for use as a highly capable and flexible photo frame.

There are several ways you can view photos on your iPad 2:

▶ One at a time, within the Photos option of the Photos app.

▶ One at a time, within an Album in the Albums option of the Photos app.

▶ One at a time, within a group of photos taken in a specific place, in the Places option of the Photos app. (Shows all geotagged photos taken in a specific place.)

▶ One at a time, within the Events or Faces option of the Photos app. (These two categories must be configured in either the iPhoto or Aperture application on a Macintosh personal computer, and then added to the iPad 2 by syncing it to the Mac. These options are not available on Windows PCs.)

▶ As a slideshow within any option of the Photos app.

▶ As screen wallpaper on the Home screen, the Lock screen, or both.

▶ Using the Picture Frame option of the Lock screen to go through all your photos, or all the photos in a given Album or other category.

Using an appropriate connector, such as those described in Lesson 1, you can display photos on a TV or projector for viewing by many people.

Follow the steps in this section to manage the display of photos on your iPad 2.

CAUTION: **Managing iPad Photos**

You cannot delete photos imported from your computer on the iPad 2, nor can you rearrange them into different folders. This is annoying when you have one or two photos that you really don't want to show a lot of people, embedded among photos that you do want to share. To manage photos imported from your computer on the iPad 2, make changes in your photo files and folders on your personal computer and then re-sync using iTunes, as described in Lesson 18.

Getting Photos as Screenshots and Attachments

Although many photos come to your iPad 2 by transferring them from your personal computer and other devices, there are two ways to get photos onto your iPad 2 that don't necessarily apply to other devices: as email attachments and as iPad 2 screenshots.

When you get an email, the photo shows up as an attachment icon in the body of the email. To download the photo, tap the icon. The photo downloads.

To save or copy the image, tap it. Options appear to enable you to save the image or copy it, as shown in Figure 14.2. (You can do the same with images on websites; be careful, though, not to violate copyright in your use of images obtained in this way.)

FIGURE 14.2   Saving images is easy.

You can also create images by taking a screenshot of whatever is on the iPad 2 screen, such as a website you are viewing. Just hold down the Home button, and then press the Sleep/Wake button. The current screen contents are captured.

For email attachments and screenshots, images are saved into the Saved Photos folder.

TIP: **Create Your Own Zoomed Photo**

Some iPad 2 features enable you to pan and zoom before saving a photo. You can also use panning and zooming to edit your photos on iPad 2. Just bring up a photo for viewing, as described in the next section. Then pan (by dragging) and zoom (by pinching) to get the appearance you want. Take a screenshot of the result and use it as a photo of its own. The resolution will be somewhat lower, depending on how much you've zoomed, but the result may still look good.

Viewing Photos

You can view photos in several ways in the Photos app. When you open the Photos app, you have the choice of viewing your photos as Photos, Albums, or Places. (They can also be viewed as Events or Faces, if you use iPhoto or Aperture on a Mac to create these categories.) The following outlines how each category works:

▶ If you choose Photos, you see a large array of photos, as shown previously in Figure 14.1.

▶ If you choose Albums, you see photos grouped by date. You can spread an Album to view the photos in it, as shown in Figure 14.3.

▶ If you choose Places, you see a map with pins showing where your geo-referenced photos were taken, as shown in Figure 14.4. (Some cameras, including some smartphone cameras, include geo-referencing information in photos automatically.) Touch a pin to see the initial photo for that location; spread the group of photos with your fingers to preview the group.

Viewing and Sharing Individual Photos

When you view an individual photo from any source, it fits the screen in its current orientation. Move the screen to a horizontal or vertical orientation as needed to best fit the photo.

The photo is shown without controls for maximum impact—when you tap the screen, controls are shown. Here are the controls available:

▶ **Zoom and pan**—You can pinch your fingers together on the screen to zoom in, unpinch to zoom back out, and then drag to pan within the picture. You can make the photo quite different just by zooming and panning around within it. You can then take a screenshot, as described later in this section, to create a new photo from the old one. This self-created shot may be useful for emailing, for instance, since you don't otherwise have the option to edit a photo before sending it.

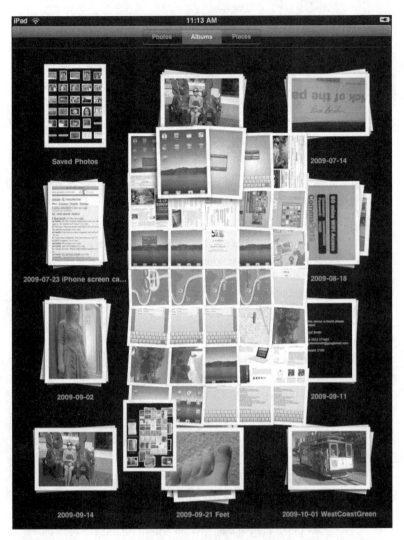

FIGURE 14.3   A set of folders, with the middle folder spread to show its contents.

▶ **Choose from photos in a folder**—To move to another photo in the same folder, tap the photo; controls appear that enable you to move to other photos, as shown in Figure 14.4. Then tap the photo you want in the strip at the bottom. (This feature is not

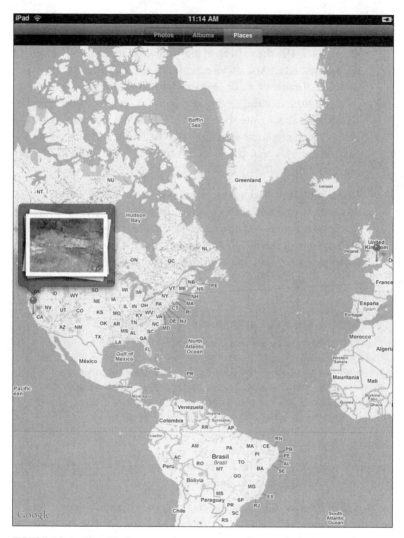

FIGURE 14.4 The Photos app gives you geo-referenced photo groupings.

very useful in folders with dozens of photos or more, which is likely to be the case for the Photos tab within the Photos app, for instance. However, you can get more selective power by pressing and holding on the strip, and then dragging the highlight slowly from one photo to the next.)

▶ **Create a slideshow**—To view a folder's photos in a slideshow, tap the Slideshow button. Slideshow options appear, as shown in Figure 14.5. Use the options to play music or not, and to choose the music to play. Also choose transition effects, such as Cube, Dissolve, Ripple, Wipe, or Origami; try them all to see which ones you like. To change other settings—the length of time each slide plays, whether the slideshow repeats, and whether to shuffle photos randomly in the slideshow—go to Settings, Photos. (The defaults are 3 seconds per slide, no repeating, and the shuffle function turned off.)

▶ **Delete a photo**—You have the option to delete the photos you take with your iPad 2. Simply select the photo and press the trash can icon. A button with the words Delete Photo appears. Press the button to delete the photo. Photos imported from iTunes, however, do not carry the same option. You must delete these on your personal computer and re-sync.

TIP: **Get the Most Out of Slideshows**

Creating slideshows can take considerable time and effort to get the folder contents right before setting up the slideshow. However, the effect of slideshows on your photos is wonderful, and even a simple slideshow with seemingly ordinary photos can be very powerful. You can also view your slideshows on various external displays with an appropriate connector for your iPad 2.

Tap the Share icon to open up additional options, as shown in Figure 14.6. The options available are as follows:

▶ **Email Photo**—An email message with the photo in it opens. You can address the email, enter a subject line, and add text.

▶ **Assign to Contact**—iPad 2 gives you a great opportunity to assign a photo to a contact. Tap Assign to Contact; then choose the contact to save the photo with. The Photo app then lets you pan and zoom the photo to select just the part that you want to assign to your contact. Click Use when you're done, and the

FIGURE 14.5   You can return to the containing folder, start a slideshow, email a photo, use other options, or move among photos in the current folder.

cropped section of the photo will be used for your contact. If you have your contacts synced to other platforms, as described in Lesson 7, "Syncing, Sending, and Receiving Email," the photo will appear on those platforms as well.

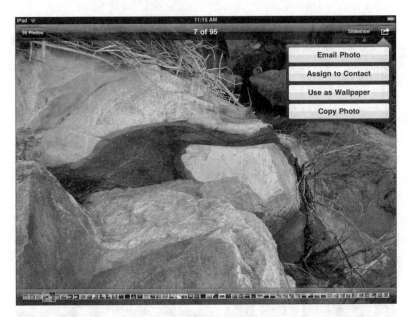

FIGURE 14.6 You have the option to email a photo, assign it to a contact, use it as wallpaper for the home or lock screens, or copy a photo.

▶ **Use as Wallpaper**—You can use a photo as wallpaper for your lock screen, your home screen, or both. Pan and zoom to get the look of the photo the way you want it; then click the appropriate Set button.

▶ **Copy Photo**—You can copy a photo for use in various applications.

▶ **Print**—Print the photo to a printer connected to your iPad 2 via AirPlay.

Using Picture Frame

Picture Frame is a novel iPad 2 application that's similar to the screensaver functionality available on many personal computers. However, the look and feel of the iPad 2 and its screen gives the photos in Picture Frame great impact.

Follow these steps to set up Picture Frame:

1. Go to Settings, Picture Frame. Picture Frame has different settings than the Photos app has.

2. Choose a transition effect: Dissolve or Origami.

3. Choose whether to zoom in on faces.

   If you turn on this option, iPad 2 finds and zooms in on faces while displaying slides in the Picture Frame.

4. Choose All Photos, or choose specific albums. Press Albums to see available albums, as shown in Figure 14.7. Choose the albums you want displayed. Clear the check marks next to the albums you don't want displayed.

5. To start or stop Picture Frame, press the Sleep/Wake button to lock your iPad 2. From the Lock screen, tap the Picture Frame button to bring the Picture Frame onscreen.

Picture Frame begins displaying photos.

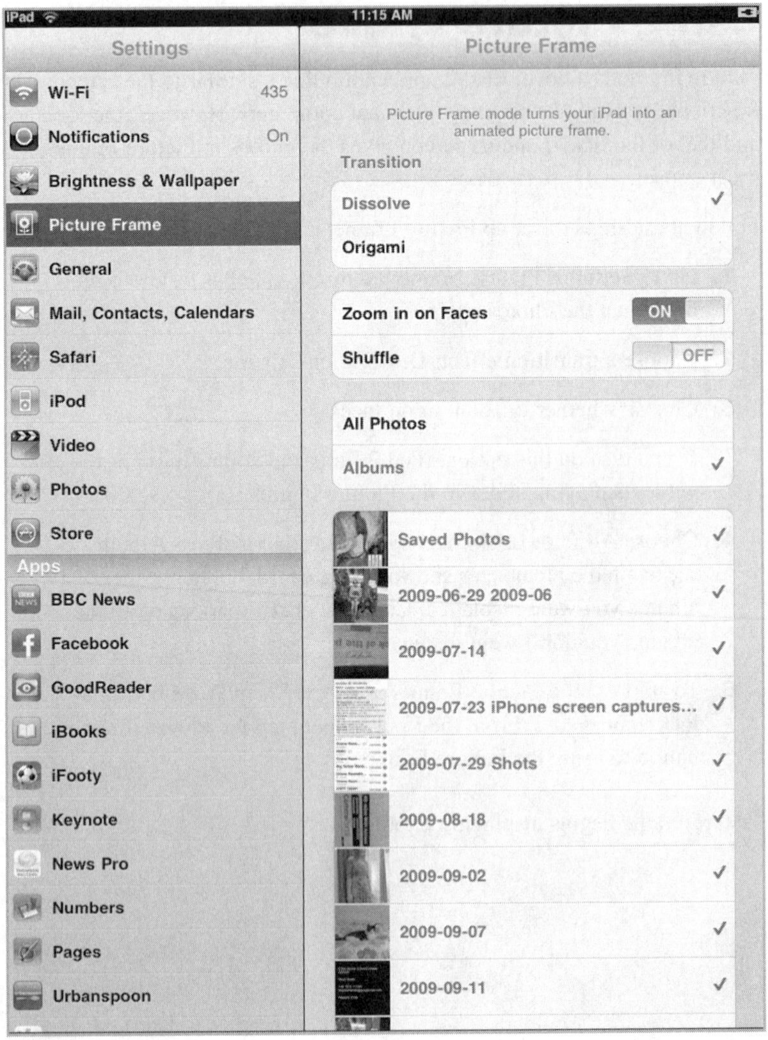

FIGURE 14.7   Picture Frame has settings of its own.

Summary

In this lesson, you learned how to use photos on the iPad 2, including importing them, taking screenshots, sharing them, and viewing them in albums and in the Picture Frame. In the next lesson, I show you how to play videos on your iPad 2.

LESSON 15

Playing Videos and YouTube

In this lesson, you learn about the many kinds of video and sources for video you can play on your iPad 2, how to play them, and how to find and play YouTube videos.

About Videos and YouTube

The progress of video seems to be going to two extremes: In many homes, large, flat-screen TVs are used to show hundreds of channels, with the selection fed by ever more expensive cable and satellite television services. On the other end of the spectrum is the iPad 2, a small, highly portable device, far less expensive to operate and with much less impact on the environment.

Many people are making greater and greater use of such a la carte video. The iPad 2 is arguably the best portable, personal device, and iTunes and YouTube among the best delivery vehicles, for this new way of accessing video.

With iPad 2, you can view many kinds of video, as follows:

▶ Movies

▶ Music videos

▶ Video podcasts

▶ TV shows

▶ Special videos created for use on digital devices

Not only can you view all of these kinds of video on your iPad 2, you can view them on your TV as well. Apple makes and sells several types of adapters that connect an iPad 2 to different kinds of TVs to echo the iPad 2 display on the TV. And if you have an Apple TV unit for your TV, you can use Apple's AirPlay service to wirelessly stream video, music, photos, and more from your iPad 2 to your TV. See Lesson 1 for details.

The videos you play on your iPad 2 are accessed several ways as well:

▶ The iTunes store, which is very efficient and has a lot of great content, especially movies and TV shows you can buy or rent. You can use iTunes to bring a wide range of content to your iPad 2.

▶ Websites, such as TV channel sites, which offer many shows for free, others for a fee.

▶ Movie and video subscription services, such as Netflix, which offer streaming services.

▶ YouTube, which includes many videos made and distributed for use on digital devices such as iPad 2.

▶ Innumerable sites with access to large or small amounts of video—some general, some specialized. Many use the emerging HTML5 standard and are referred to as HTML5 video-enabled websites. Many others use Flash, however, and don't work on the iPad 2, although this is steadily changing as more sites add HTML5 support.

This lesson explains how to find videos, how to play videos stored on your iPad 2, and how to play videos from the YouTube site.

Playing Videos

One thing to be aware of when using videos on iPad 2 is the considerable amount of time it takes to download video to your personal computer, or directly to your iPad 2. It's hardly "instant gratification." Even with a broadband connection, it can easily take about half the time to download a video that it takes to watch it. So, for a two-hour movie, plan on the download taking approximately an hour.

You need to plan your video purchases or rentals in advance, so that the downloading is completed before you're ready to watch.

If you download the video to your personal computer first, you can either stream it to your iPad 2 using AirPlay or copy it to your iPad 2. Copying it to your iPad 2 saves you time, but takes up precious storage space.

TIP: **Save Your Rental Time**

When downloading a rental, be aware that the rental time period doesn't start until you actually start playing the movie. So don't start playing it back just to check that it works. Instead, wait until you're ready to watch at least a good part of the video.

Another constraint to consider when buying or renting video content is the limited amount of storage space on the iPad 2—roughly a tenth to a fourth of what you'll find on a typical personal computer. The best strategy for managing this issue is to store videos on your personal computer and then use AirPlay to stream them to your iPad wirelessly—without affecting storage space on your iPad 2—or sync them to your iPad 2 selectively. See Lesson 18, "Using iTunes and Home Sharing," for information on how to get videos for your iPad 2 and then stream them or sync them to the device.

TIP: **Store Your Videos on Your Computer**

When you're on a shared network, you can access movies stored in iTunes on your Windows or Macintosh personal computer using iTunes Home Sharing. You first turn the feature on in iTunes (see Lesson 18). After that's done, playing back videos in the Videos app is easy and flexible. It takes a few seconds for a show to start, but after that, performance is very close to what you would expect for a video stored on your iPad 2. You need to transfer movies to your iPad 2 only if you want to watch them away from home.

After you have a video on your iPad 2, playing it back is easy:

   1. Tap Videos to start the app.

2. Choose a category that has videos in it, such as Movies or TV Shows.

   The available videos display, including any videos stored on your personal computer that are available via Home Sharing (see Lesson 18). Related videos may be grouped together, and longer videos may be grouped into chapters. For instance, if you have several episodes of a TV show, an icon showing the TV show, not the individual episodes, may display.

3. If necessary, tap the icon for a group of videos, such as episodes in a TV series.

   The individual episodes display. An example is shown in Figure 15.1.

4. To play the video, tap its icon.

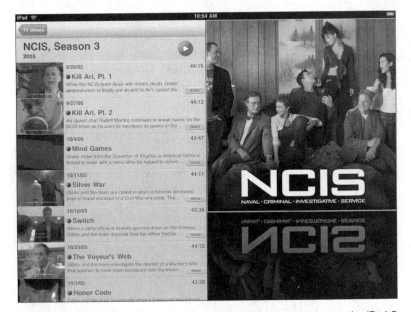

FIGURE 15.1   You can store an entire series of a favorite show on the iPad 2.

5. To control the video, tap the screen. The controls for the video display, as shown in Figure 15.2. To hide the controls, tap the screen again, or wait a few seconds and they will disappear on their own.

FIGURE 15.2 The iPad 2 displays control functions onscreen.

6. You can tap Pause to stop the video and then tap Play to resume playing it. Press and hold the Rewind or Fast Forward icons to move to the beginning or end of the video or chapter; or drag the volume slider at the bottom of the screen to change the playback volume.

7. To get to a specific spot in the video, drag the slider along the top to the spot you want. This slider is called the "scrubber bar," and you can slow down its speed of movement—the "scrub rate"—by dragging your finger from the scrubber bar down the screen. When you reach the bottom of the screen, the scrub rate slows to nearly a frame-by-frame rate.

8. You can also pause a video without using its controls in order to do something else on your iPad 2, such as read an email. While a video is playing, tap Home and open a different app. The video pauses. When you return to it, it will resume where you left off.

9. When you're finished watching the video, tap Done. The screen returns to the list of videos that contains the video you were watching.

10. To delete a video, press and hold its icon until the X button appears for deleting it. Tap the X button.

   The video is deleted from iPad 2, but will remain available for redownload or transfer from your personal computer via iTunes. See Lesson 18 for details.

NOTE: **Watch on a Bigger Screen**

To watch videos or YouTube from your iPad 2 on a computer monitor, TV, or projector, use an Apple VGA Adapter, Apple Component AV Cable, Apple Composite AV Cable, or Apple Digital AV Adapter, which are described in Lesson 1.

Finding and Playing YouTube Videos

YouTube is an amazing resource for videos. It contains a great deal of recent cultural history—including broadcast videos (or clips from them), in addition to videos recorded primarily for use with YouTube or other online sites.

You can use YouTube only if you have an active Internet connection. So, if you plan to watch videos while away from reliable Internet access, they must first be downloaded.

Some features of YouTube will work better for you if you have a YouTube account. To sign up for an account, visit the YouTube site at www.youtube. com. (On the iPad 2, you need to sign up for your YouTube account in a web browser. The YouTube site's full capabilities cannot be accessed through the YouTube app.)

There are several ways to get to YouTube videos on your iPad 2:

▶ **Web site embedding**—Many videos on different websites are hosted on YouTube, but you see them embedded in the website you're visiting.

▶ **Web site links**—Many websites link to videos for playback on the YouTube site, either in conjunction with embedding them on the site with the link, or only via the link.

▶ **The YouTube site**—Visit the YouTube site in your web browser and play back videos there. The YouTube app offers easier access to YouTube features, particularly if you have a YouTube account.

▶ **The YouTube app**—YouTube is a built-in app on every iPad 2. It doesn't do many of the things that the YouTube site does, but it's very easy to use.

▶ **Search**—Search is really powerful on YouTube. If you don't believe me, just try a search for "skateboard dog," and be prepared to spend half an hour or so laughing at videos of dogs on skateboards.

▶ **Categories**—The YouTube app offers easy access to several categories of videos: Featured videos, Top Rated, Most Viewed, Favorites that you've marked, and a History of videos you've viewed, among others. You are also offered access to features that require you to have an account: Your subscriptions and videos you've created and uploaded to YouTube (My Videos).

▶ **Related videos**—After you find and play back a video, YouTube offers easy access to related videos. This is probably the leading feature of YouTube that entices people to spend hours watching YouTube videos when they should be doing something—almost anything—else.

CAUTION: **Connect to the Internet for YouTube**

You can use YouTube only when you have an Internet connection, and a slow or intermittent Internet connection may cause problems with video playback.

Playing a YouTube video is similar to playing a stored video, as described in the previous section, but with a few differences. Here's a brief overview:

▶ **Short videos**—YouTube videos are more limited in length. YouTube generally has a 10-minute limit, and most videos are much shorter than that.

▶ **Internet access matters**—Spotty Internet access will cause problems with video playback, and no Internet access means no YouTube access, either via the YouTube app or the YouTube website.

▶ **Landscape rules**—Watch YouTube videos with your iPad 2 in landscape mode for best effect.

▶ **Full Screen is an option**—The usual YouTube display shows a video, comments about it, and related videos (see Figure 15.3).

FIGURE 15.3   YouTube offers lots of related content and options.

To see just the video, tap the Full Screen button. The video fills the screen.

▶ **View/Hide controls**—During video playback, the controls disappear so that you can see the video fully. Tap the screen to see controls, and tap it again to hide them.

▶ **Favoritize frequently**—Add a video to your Favorites by tapping the Favorites button.

▶ **Email a link**—Use the Email control to email a video link to a friend. Add the email address, the subject, and/or desired comments, and send.

▶ **See Related videos, More From the video's maker, and Comments**—Tap the appropriate button to access these additional features.

▶ **Rate or leave a Comment**—Tap Rate to rate a video and/or add a comment. (You have to be logged into an account to rate or comment on videos.)

▶ **Subscribe**—If you're logged in to your account, you can subscribe to videos from the current video's maker.

Summary

In this lesson, you learned about the many kinds of video and sources for video you can play on your iPad 2, how to play them, and how to find and play YouTube videos. In the next lesson, I show you how to use the iPod app to manage music.

LESSON 16

Using iPad 2 for Music and More

In this lesson, you learn about how music works on iPad 2 and how to play music, podcasts, and audiobooks, as well as how to create regular and Genius playlists.

Playing Music and Other Audio Files

The iPad 2's music app is called iPod, and the app works just like an iPod device. The iPod—whether it's the physical device or the app—is not really complete in and of itself. It's just one crucial element in a system that allows music and other audio content to be created, distributed—sometimes for free, sometimes for a price—played back, and managed.

To play audio files from the iPad 2 app, you can use four different means:

- ▶ **iPad 2's built-in speakers**—The iPad 2 has a built-in speaker that, considering its small size and thinness, produces surprisingly good sound.

- ▶ **External speakers**—External speakers produce better results through their larger size and, for two-piece stereo speakers, greater separation. The iPad 2 Dock (described in Lesson 1, "Introducing iPad 2") has an audio line-out port that enables you to connect to external speakers.

- ▶ **Wired headphones**—Headphones give even better results than speakers by bringing the sound closer to your ears and providing stereo separation, especially because the best (and most expensive) headphones also cut out ambient noise. Even simple, inexpensive wired headphones give surprisingly good sound. You can plug just the audio jack of audio/microphone combo headphones into the iPad 2's audio-out jack and get sound. However, somewhat more expensive wired headphones from Apple and others give noticeably better sound.

▶ **Wireless Bluetooth headphones**—Wireless Bluetooth headphones can be paired to the iPad 2, as described in Lesson 4, "Getting Connected to Wi-Fi, 3G, and Bluetooth." Even the less-expensive wireless headphones give you a great deal of freedom and flexibility, and more advanced headphones with features like noise cancellation provide excellent sound.

Finding a Song by Category

To play a song, you first need to get to its icon in iPad 2, as follows:

1. Tap the iPod icon to start the app.

2. Choose a category that has audio in it, such as Music, Podcasts, or Audiobooks. You can also use the buttons at the bottom to look in categories—Songs, Artists, Albums, Genres, and Composers.

3. Tap the icon for an album, if needed, to see the songs that belong to it.

4. Tap the icon for a song.

    The song plays, displaying the album cover art, as shown in Figure 16.1.

TIP: **Keeping Music Alive**
Music playback is supported by background services in iOS. You can press the Home button to find and use another app; your audio continues playing.

Finding a Song by Searching

You can also find a song by searching for it:

1. Tap the Search box. Tap X to clear any previous entries.

FIGURE 16.1   Finding and playing songs on the iPad 2 is easy.

The onscreen keyboard opens to allow you to enter search text.

Enter something to search on. It can be a word from the song title or album, or the name of the artist or composer. Spelling matters, but capitalization doesn't. Search does not work inside names, only starting at the beginning of a name—for instance, "ach" won't find Bach, although "bac" will.

If no valid results are found, the words "No Results" will display—even before you tap Search.

2. Tap the Search button on the keyboard to clear the keyboard and display final results.

The search might find valid results in any of the categories: Songs, Artists, Albums, Genres, or Composers. (For instance, a search for "Mothers" might find both the recording artists, the Mothers of Invention, and the composer Mark Mothersbaugh of Devo.) The categories in which valid results are found among your music selection are shown in normal text, and the categories in which no valid results are found are shown in grayed-out text.

You see results immediately if the category you had selected before the search began has valid search results; you see the words "No Results" if none of the categories has a valid result.

3. Tap category names that aren't grayed-out to view results.

Results are displayed, as shown in Figure 16.2.

FIGURE 16.2   Search helps you find your songs.

TIP: **Search with Short Strings**

Begin your search by entering just three or four letters of a search string. Unless you have an astoundingly large music collection, a short string is often enough to bring up your desired result.

Playing Back Songs

While a song is playing back, the Now Playing screen appears, as shown in Figure 16.3. This control gives you several options, as follows:

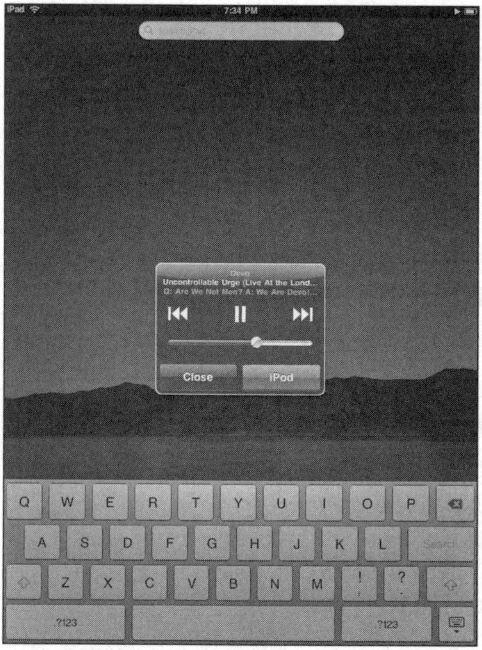

FIGURE 16.3   Podcasts and audiobooks have additional controls.

▶ **Volume**—Use the slider in the upper-left corner of the iPad 2 screen or the physical volume control on your iPad 2 to change the volume. You may also have a volume control on your headphones, which may or may not override the volume controls for your iPad 2. Experiment with all the controls to see how they interact.

▶ **Pause/Play**—When a song is playing, the Pause control appears; when you tap Pause, the Play control replaces it.

▶ **Advance/Rewind**—On either side of the Pause/Play controls, the Rewind and Advance controls are available. Tap Rewind to start at the song's beginning, and then tap repeatedly to move back through previous songs. Tap Advance to move to the beginning of the next song, and tap it again to move through subsequent songs.

▶ **Move ahead/back**—During playback, a round ball indicates the current location of playback in the song. Drag the ball backward or forward to move to a different spot in the song.

- ▶ **Playback list**—Tap the album art icon in the main list to see a playlist. Tap beside the playlist to return to seeing the album art icon in the main list.

- ▶ **Album art**—Tap the album art icon under Now Playing to see it full size. Pinch the full-size album art to return to the usual playback screen.

Playing Back Podcasts and Audiobooks

While a podcast or audiobook is playing back, additional controls appear, as shown in Figure 16.3:

- ▶ **Repeat**—Tap to repeat the content indefinitely.

- ▶ **Scrubbing**—As with videos (see Lesson 15, "Playing Videos and YouTube"), you can change the rate of forwarding or rewinding, an action referred to as "scrubbing." This is done by dragging your finger down the screen as you move it ahead of or behind the current play point in the content.

- ▶ **Playback speed**—Tap the 1x button to change the playback speed among 1x, 2x, and 1/2x. Normally, fast playback makes speech high-pitched and unpleasant, but the iPod app automatically adjusts the pitch to make the audio easy to listen to, even at high speeds.

- ▶ **Skip**—You can skip back in the content by a predefined amount by tapping the Skip button.

Using Playlists

Playlists are collections you make of your own songs. You can use them to create a mood, to power a party, or for any other purpose you can think of. Playlists are one of the secrets of the success of the iPod device and the iPod capability on the iPhone and iPad 2.

A Genius playlist is a special feature that creates playlists by searching for songs that go well together. The Genius feature works best if you have a large and eclectic playlist—so large that you don't even get around to playing some of your songs. A Genius playlist will often dig up these undiscovered gems, mixing them with other songs in interesting ways.

Creating Playlists

Although you may put a lot of thought into choosing and ordering the songs in a playlist, the actual steps you need to follow to create the list are easy, as follows:

1. In the iPod app, tap + at the bottom of the screen.

2. Enter a name for the playlist, and then tap Save.

   The iPod app lists all your songs.

3. Tap the + button to add a song to your playlist. Alternatively, you can look in Artists, Albums, Genres, or Composers to find songs to add. Tap Sources to browse among different kinds of sources, as shown in Figure 16.4.

FIGURE 16.4   Playlists can draw on all your sources.

4. Tap Done when finished. The next time you sync with your personal computer, your playlist will be saved in iTunes as well.

5. To edit the playlist, tap Edit, and then drag the box next to each selection to move it up or down in the list. Tap the minus sign (–) next to the selection to remove it; tap Add Songs and tap the + button next to songs to add them, or tap the minus sign (–) next to the playlist name to remove the entire playlist. See Figure 16.5 for an example of a playlist being edited.

FIGURE 16.5   Playlists are easy to edit.

Creating Genius Playlists

To use the Genius function, you need to first turn on the Genius function in iTunes. In iTunes, look for the Genius icon in the left tray. Click the icon to turn on the feature; for details, see Lesson 18.

After the Genius feature is enabled, creating a Genius playlist is easy. Just tap the Genius button—the atomic-looking button shown in Figure 16.5—

and then tap New. Choose a song in the list. Genius creates a playlist of similar songs from your collection. Tap Save; the playlist is created, with the name of the song that you were viewing when you created it.

You can refresh your Genius playlist to incorporate different songs or new songs that you've added to your collection. Simply tap Refresh in the Genius playlist. You can also delete Genius playlists.

The process sounds kind of random, but people with large song collections often report surprising success with Genius.

Genius also searches your iPad 2 library and creates Genius Mixes, each of which taps into a different type of music. To play a Genius Mix, just tap its name.

Summary

In this lesson, you learned how to play music, podcasts, and audiobooks on your iPad 2, as well as how to create regular and Genius playlists. In the next lesson, I show you how to use iBooks and the iBookstore.

LESSON 17

Using iBooks and the iBookstore

In this lesson, you learn about reading iBooks on your iPad 2 and using the iBookstore and other sources to get free and paid-for books for your iPad 2.

Introducing iBooks

The iBooks app is the iPad 2's book-reading software. An iBook is a book specially formatted for use in the iBooks app on the iPad 2. Unlike a printed book, an iBook can contain multimedia content such as video clips; however, to date, not many of them do.

There's a lot of excitement about iBooks for many reasons. One important reason is the size, shape, and weight of the iPad 2. The device is quite light—several ounces lighter than the original iPad—and the screen size is quite similar to the page size of many books. Another reason is the large, bright, colorful screen of the iPad 2, all adorning a device meant to be held in one's hands, like a book. You, as the reader, can get as close to the content as you want, without strain. You can experience full-color illustrations, animations, and video, unlike many of the e-reading devices available today. You can also stay connected to email, social media networks, and other digital tools while reading.

Adversely, the weight of the iPad 2, at one and a third pounds, is still about 30% heavier than a typical 300-page softcover book.

Like other electronic devices used for reading, the iPad 2 offers great search capabilities—a feature readers of printed books have long wished for. However, unlike most other e-reading devices, with iPad 2 you also have access to the full Internet experience on the same device as your e-books. An e-book can link to the Internet, incorporate Internet content, be updated over the Internet, and much more.

You can buy books to use with the iBooks app directly from your iPad 2 or from iTunes running on your personal computer. Synchronizing the iBooks app and iTunes copies the book from your iPad 2 to the iTunes software running on your PC, or vice versa. See Lesson 18, "Using tunes and Home Sharing," for details.

As described more fully in the "Finding and Buying Books" section later in this lesson, you can also get books in ePub format, a widely used industry standard, to use in iBooks. Many book reader programs and browser add-ons for personal computers support ePub, as do devices such as the Sony Reader, the Barnes and Noble Nook e-book reader, and phones and devices using Google's Android operating system. You can drag and drop ePub books into iTunes on your computer, and you can then sync them to your iPad 2, as described in Lesson 18.

TIP: **Get the iBooks App First**

Your iPad 2 does not, at this writing, come with the free iBooks app installed. Find the iBooks app in the App Store, and download and install it before proceeding. See Lesson 12 for information on getting apps.

Comparing iBooks to Alternatives

You may want to download the iBooks app for reading books on your iPad 2. There are a few books that are available only on iBooks, and most reviews—as well as my own experience—rate the iBooks reading experience as a little smoother and easier on the eyes, better than alternatives.

However, there is a disadvantage to the iBooks app: It's iPad-only. If you also want to read a given book on other devices, you will probably want to consider alternative book-reading apps in addition to iBooks. The most popular alternatives are Amazon's Kindle and the Nook from Barnes and Noble.

Both Kindle and Nook are available as hardware devices, as personal computer software, and as apps for smartphones and tablet computers, including the iPad 2. If you stop reading at a given page on one device, you pick up on the same page when you open the book on another device.

Both Kindle and Nook offer books that iBooks doesn't. iBooks has some unique titles as well, but fewer than the other two. Although all three are growing their base of titles rapidly, there are also books being published for only one of the platforms—especially Kindle.

Consider installing the Kindle and/or Nook apps—either right away, as a preemptive measure, or when you can't find the book you want on iBooks. Using the competing apps is much like using iBooks, so the lessons you learn on iBooks will transfer easily to the competition.

Reading Books

Follow these steps to read an iBook:

1. Press the iBooks icon to start the app.

2. Find the book you want to read; then tap to open it.

   After it's open, you see either the cover, the Table of Contents, the first page of content, or a page to which the book was previously open.

3. To get a feel for the look of the book as it would appear if it were a physical book in your hands, hold the iPad 2 horizontally. To fill the screen with a somewhat larger view of a single page, hold the iPad 2 vertically.

   The look changes as you move from horizontal to vertical. Doing this is important for illustrated books and other books with carefully laid-out page spreads, such as the *Winnie the Pooh* book that you can download for free.

4. To scroll through the book's pages one at a time, swipe to the left or right.

5. To bookmark a word, or look it up in the Dictionary, or use it for searching, press and hold the word. (You don't bookmark a page or a paragraph in iBooks; you bookmark a specific word.)

The word is highlighted, and a menu of options appears: Dictionary, Bookmark, and Search, as shown in Figure 17.1. The Dictionary option brings up a definition of the word. However, the definition may not be aligned with what you're reading; for instance, looking up the name "Christopher" while reading *Winnie the Pooh* brings up a reference to the late former U.S. Secretary of State Warren Christopher, but nothing about Christopher Robin. Searching brings up a list of all references to that word in the currently open book, as described in steps 15 and 16.

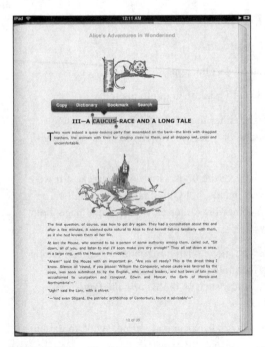

FIGURE 17.1   Start by selecting to look up a word in the Dictionary, Bookmark it, or Search for it.

6. Choose the Bookmark option to bookmark the word. The word then appears in yellow highlighter color, and a bookmark to the word is added to the Bookmarks list.

7. To change the bookmark color of a bookmarked word, or to change the bookmarking color for that word and subsequent bookmarks, press and hold on the word. Choose Unbookmark to remove the word from the bookmarks list. To change the color highlighting of that word, choose the new bookmarking color from the list that appears.

8. To prevent the page from flipping between horizontal and vertical mode, get the screen display the way you like it and turn on the Screen Rotation Lock on the side of your iPad 2.

The screen won't rotate again until you turn off the Screen Rotation Lock. This works only if you have the switch set to serve as a Screen Rotation Lock rather than a Mute switch; see Lesson 5 for details.

9. To see controls, if they're not already visible, tap the screen.

Controls appear across the top of the screen, as shown in Figure 17.2. You can always make controls disappear and reappear by tapping the screen.

10. To return to the Library, tap the Library button in the upper-left corner. This closes the book and reopens the Library.

11. To bring up the Table of Contents, tap the Table of Contents button located next to the Library button.

The Table of Contents appears, as shown in Figure 17.3. A Resume button appears. You can press the Resume button to return to your previous page. The Resume button disappears when you return to the content.

12. To move directly into the book from the Table of Contents, tap any entry.

13. To switch to the Bookmarks list, tap the Table of Contents button at the top of the page to return to the page shown in Figure

17.2. Tap the Bookmarks button, and then choose a bookmark. Alternatively, press Resume to return to your former place in the book.

To see all the entries in a long Table of Contents or Bookmarks list, drag to scroll up and down.

14. To change the brightness level, tap the Brightness button in the upper-right corner.

A slider appears that enables you to change the brightness level.

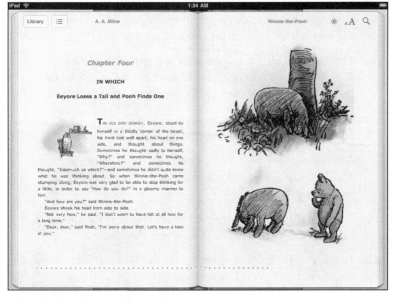

FIGURE 17.2   Reading books, like playing songs, is easy and fun.

TIP: **iBooks-Specific Brightness**

The iBooks Brightness feature is available in iBooks only, and applies only to your use of iBooks. When you leave the iBooks app, your iBooks brightness setting will be ignored.

---

15. To change the font and font size, tap the Font button located in the upper-right corner.

You're presented with controls to make the font size bigger and smaller, as shown in Figure 17.4. As you make changes, the text reflows to suit your preferences.

FIGURE 17.3   The Table of Contents and Bookmarks features give you quick access to the book's content.

16. To search for a specific word in the book, tap the Search icon. Enter a search term in the window that appears, and then tap the Search button in the onscreen keyboard.

A list of search results for the iBook appears. To search on a term you find in the text instead, press and hold it; then choose Search from the options that appear.

17. To continue your search on the Web (Internet connection required), change the search terms if needed, and then press the Search Google button or the Search Wikipedia button at the bottom of the search box.

The Safari web browser opens, and search results appear. Google searches the entire Web, whereas Wikipedia searches only the Wikipedia online dictionary.

FIGURE 17.4   You can easily change fonts and sizes.

18. To scroll through the book's pages quickly, use the slider at the bottom of the screen.

TIP: **Saving Your Page in iBooks**

You can keep your place in a book and still close it to return to the Library, or press the Home button to return to the Home screen. When you return to your book, it opens to the page you were on most recently. To start the book fresh when you return, use the slider to go back to the front cover or Table of Contents before you exit the book.

Using the Bookshelf

You can use the Bookshelf to browse your books or to delete a book. Follow these steps to work with the Bookshelf:

1. Tap the iBooks app icon to start it. If the app opens to a book rather than the Bookshelf, tap the Library button to return to the Bookshelf.

2. Tap the list button to sort your books, and then select a sorting criterion from among the options on the bottom of the screen: Titles, Authors, and Categories (such as fiction). The books are sorted and displayed in a list, as shown in Figure 17.5. Push the Bookshelf button to return to the Bookshelf.

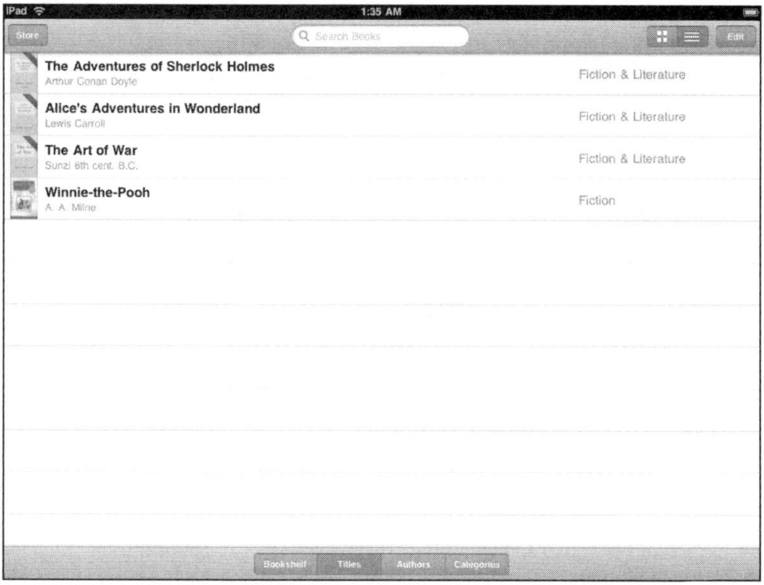

FIGURE 17.5 Books in your Library can be displayed in a list.

3. Tap the Bookshelf view button to return to viewing your books in the Bookshelf.

4. To delete a book from the Bookshelf, tap Edit, or press and hold on any book's cover until the books start to shake. Tap each book that you want to delete to select it. Then tap the Delete button, and the books disappear. Then tap Edit again or press Home. The books stop shaking, and the delete (X button) control disappears from the book icons.

If in the future, you change your mind about a book you've previously deleted, and you've synced your iPad 2 to your personal computer, you can redownload the book to iPad 2 from iTunes on your personal computer. If the book you deleted was obtained via iBookstore, you can download it again from the Purchases tab in the Bookstore, as described later in this lesson.

NOTE: **Deleting Books from the Bookshelf**

When you delete a book from your Bookshelf, it will always be available for redownload to your iPad 2, either by syncing with iTunes on your personal computer or from the Purchases tab in the iBookstore. This enables you to delete any books you want from the Bookshelf on your iPad 2 without fear of thereby permanently losing them.

Finding and Buying Books

Books for iBooks on the iPad 2 can be accessed in three ways:

▶ From the iPad 2, you can get books from iBookstore. You can't get books from websites, as email attachments, or by any other means.

▶ From your personal computer, one way to get books is to buy the book through iTunes. It's then transferred to your iPad 2 the next time you sync; see Lesson 18 for details.

▶ Also from your personal computer, you can get books in ePub format by downloading them from websites, as email attachments, and so on. Then drag and drop the ePub-formatted file into iTunes. The book is transferred to your iPad 2 the next time you sync; see Lesson 18 for details.

TIP: **Getting Free Books**

Many free books are available directly from the iBookstore, including the huge catalog of more than 40,000 free, out-of-copyright books from Project Gutenberg (www.gutenberg.org), which showcases many classics. The most-downloaded free books are listed via the Top Charts button of iBookstore. There are, in addition, many free books available in the ePub format, but many of these books are not available directly from the iBookstore. You have to download such books on your personal computer and then use iTunes to sync them to your iPad 2, as described in the next lesson.

The sections that follow describe all of these ways to get books.

Finding Books in iBookstore

To find a book in iBookstore, tap the Store button from the Bookshelf. iBookstore will open, as shown in Figure 17.6.

FIGURE 17.6   iBookstore offers a wide range of books, many for free.

Use the following means to find books:

▶ **Search**—Enter a word from a book name or author name and tap Search on the keyboard to search for it.

▶ **New & Notable**—A short list of New & Notable books appears on the home screen of iBookstore, as shown in Figure 17.6. To see the entire list, tap the arrows, or tap the See All link.

▶ *New York Times* **bestsellers**—Tap the icon at the bottom of the screen to access the books in the *New York Times* bestseller list (fiction and nonfiction categories).

▶ **Top Charts**—Top Charts has lists of top paid-for and free books.

▶ **Purchases**—The Purchases list includes books you've downloaded for free. You can use this list to redownload books you've
previously downloaded and then deleted, whether paid for or not.

TIP: **Stock Up on Free Books Now**

Stock up iBookshelf with free books early on, so you have something
to read when your iPad 2 is out of range of an Internet connection.

Finding Books on a Personal Computer

On a personal computer, you can buy, or download for free, a number of
books in ePub format and then transfer them to your iPad 2 via iTunes.
The ePub format is an open format that does not contain copy protection,
so ePub-formatted files can be freely copied. This is different from
iBookstore books, which are copy protected.

Two of the many sites that have ePub-formatted books are as follows:

▶ **ManyBooks.net**—Includes tons of free books, with recommen-
dations and reviews.

▶ **iBookstore.com**—This is not Apple's iBookstore, available from
iPad 2, but rather, an independent website. It includes free books
in ePub format for your iPad 2, as well as free books and free
book readers for your personal computer and many cell phones.

To get ePub files into your iTunes library, you must first get the file onto
your personal computer. Then drag and drop the file into iTunes, or select
Add to Library from the iTunes application's File menu and locate the file
on your computer. The next time you sync to your iPad 2, the books will
be added to your iPad 2 Bookshelf.

Summary

In this lesson, you learned about reading iBooks on your iPad 2 and about
how to use the iBookstore and other sources to get free and paid-for books
for your iPad 2. In the next lesson, I describe how to use iTunes to sync
multimedia and much more.

LESSON 18

Using iTunes and Home Sharing

In this lesson, you learn about iTunes and how it works on the iPad 2 as well as personal computers; how to get content for the iPad 2, including music, movies, and much more; and how to use iTunes to stream data over a home wireless network and to sync your iPad 2 with a personal computer.

Understanding iTunes

iTunes is the funnel for all of Apple's content deals with music producers, Hollywood moguls, book publishers, and others, plus access to free content and user-generated content, delivering, syncing, and managing all sorts of items across devices.

As one example of its importance, through iTunes, Apple has been able to enforce a strong, but reasonably user-friendly, digital rights management (DRM) policy for some content, such as movies and some music files. (Some files are DRM-free and can be copied onto any number of devices.) For instance, it may be that no music producer would have ever come up with the idea of having up to five computers authorized to play a piece of music that had only been paid for once—but that's the limit Apple insisted on, and it stuck.

The iTunes interface is a bit odd, not even truly Mac-like in some ways. That's because the original iTunes software was built outside Apple and then acquired by Apple in a buyout of the company that made it. Apple has improved iTunes over the years, and even brought the software onto the iPhone and iPad 2, but never really overhauled it. This makes it visually and operationally different from anything else you see on the Mac—or on Windows as well. But iTunes, along with all the content you can access through it, is one of the secrets of the iPad family's early success and its continuing usefulness.

Getting Content for the iPad 2

One way to get content you want for your iPad 2 is to use the iTunes app on the iPad 2, rather than the iTunes app on your personal computer. That way, you only have to wait for the download to your iPad 2 to complete before you can use the content. If you get the content on your personal computer first, you have to wait for that download and then wait for it to sync before you see the content on your iPad 2.

However, with the introduction of iPad 2, Apple also introduced iTunes Home Sharing. With iTunes Home Sharing, you can stream content wirelessly from a personal computer to any iPad, iPhone, or iPod touch on the same network; the actual media file stays on the personal computer. If you use home sharing, it makes sense to have your personal computer as the hub for movie files, especially TV shows and movies. For more information, see the section on Home Sharing later in this lesson.

Learning how to use the iTunes app on your iPad 2 also prepares you to operate for longer periods without connecting your iPad 2 to a personal computer at all. I believe that as people get more used to the iPad 2, it may become the main or only device for some people who couldn't imagine going without a personal computer today.

For now, though, you will still want to sync content downloaded onto your iPad 2 to your personal computer. This enables you to delete content from the iPad 2, knowing you can always get it back relatively quickly by transferring it from your personal computer. You could always download it from iTunes again to your iPad 2, without cost, but that's a more time-consuming process than syncing with iTunes on your personal computer, or streaming it wirelessly after the content is already there.

NOTE: **Getting All Your Content**
Some types of content can't be accessed directly through iPad 2. This includes content that was purchased or downloaded through iTunes before purchasing your iPad 2, and audio content that you

bring into iTunes from CDs. Both scenarios are covered in the section on syncing, which you'll find later in this lesson. ePad-formatted e-books that you want to use in iBooks (outlined in Lesson 17, "Using iBooks and the iBookstore") are another type of content that can't be accessed directly through the iPad 2.

Finding Content

All the major types of content for the iPad 2—music, movies, TV shows, podcasts, audiobooks, and courseware (iTunes U)—have their own buttons at the bottom of the iTunes screen, as shown in Figure 18.1, and all work in almost the same way.

FIGURE 18.1   The iTunes app is like six stores in one for Music, Movies, TV Shows, Podcasts, Audiobooks, and iTunes U courseware.

Use the buttons at the bottom of the screen to bring up what is basically a separate iTunes Store for each particular category. Then, if you choose

Music, Movies, or TV shows, you'll be offered a choice of four buttons on the top, as shown previously for TV Shows in Figure 18.1:

> TIP: **Podcasts Come in Audio and Video**
> Podcasts can be either audio-only (the original definition) or video podcasts with audio, marked with a video icon. In fact, video podcasts are now so prevalent that it can sometimes seem difficult to find a good audio-only podcast.

▶ **Genres**—A genre is a type of content, style, or format similar to the categories you might find in a record or video store. Genres are also used for hits charts and in industry publications and websites. Use the Genres button for each type of content to see what is available.

▶ **Featured**—This is content that's hot, up and coming, of particular interest, or receiving a lot of promotional support from the publisher or artist. (And yes, there might be money changing hands to help determine what gets featured.) Looking at the Featured list is a good way to keep up with what people are talking about.

▶ **Top Charts**—Charts are not always reliable—for instance, music charts cover only a fraction of what's downloaded on the Internet—but they can be interesting. Use the charts to make sure you aren't missing anything that's broadly popular and that you might like.

▶ **Genius**—The Genius feature works with music files you already have in iTunes to find other content you might like—often reaching across genre boundaries.

Each of these four categories are available for Music, Movies, and TV Shows. Podcasts and Audiobooks don't include the Genius capability. Also, the Genres button is called Categories for these two applications, although it still does basically the same thing. At this writing, iBooks and the iBookstore lack both Genius and a Genres/Categories button, so they have only Featured and Top Charts.

The Downloads button takes you to the iPod app and opens the Purchased area; see Lesson 16, "Using iPad 2 for Music and More," for details.

> NOTE: **iBookstore Requires Separate Searches**
>
> Searching the iTunes store does go across many content types, but it doesn't include books, except for audiobooks. You need to search the iBookstore separately, as described in Lesson 17.

Finding Content in and Across Types

You can find content *within* a type—Music, Movies, TV Shows, Podcasts, Audiobooks, and iTunes U courseware—by pressing the content type button at the bottom. You then look at Genres (or Categories, for Podcasts and Audiobooks, with no similar choice for iTunes U); Featured; Top Charts; or Genius (for Music, Movies, and TV Shows).

You can also find content *across* types —with "hits" in all applicable categories—by using Search. Enter search terms in the Search area in the upper-right corner and tap Search on the keyboard. Figure 18.2 shows search results for Shakespeare, which is a term that appears in multiple categories.

You can alternate between searching within categories and using the Search function to search across categories. Each type of searching can give you ideas for the other. For instance, your interest in a given musical artist's recordings could also lead to a movie, TV show, or even a course related to that artist or their genre.

When you find an item of interest, tap it to see more information. You can also read reviews, write a review for content you own, or send an email with a link to the item. You can buy, download, or rent the item, depending on what options are available for it. (Remember that rental terms don't begin counting until you start playing the item.)

> CAUTION: **Downloads Can Be Slow**
>
> Downloading an item can take a significant amount of time. In testing on a relatively slow broadband connection, it took me a bit less than one-fourth the playing time to download music, and a bit more

than one-half the playing time to download video. Check on your own system when downloading so you know just how quickly you can get a music album downloaded before a party, or a video download before you have a friend over for movie night.

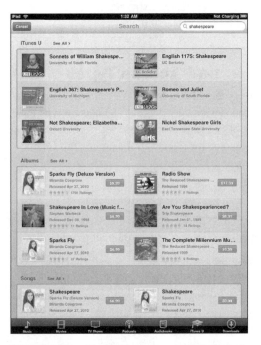

FIGURE 18.2   Shakespeare is a real king of all media.

Downloading or Purchasing Content

Before buying or downloading music, movies, TV shows, or audiobooks, you need an iTunes Store account. You also need an iTunes Store account to write reviews for any content. To get an iTunes Store account, or to switch among different iTunes Store accounts on your iPad 2, open the Settings app and tap Store. You'll then be invited to switch to a different iTunes store account or create a new account.

Purchasing content (or downloading free content) is very similar to downloading an app, as described in Lesson 12, "Getting Apps from the App

Store." You tap Install or the price. If the option is offered, tap Buy. For certain videos, you'll have to specify standard definition (480p) or high definition (720p) as well. You'll be asked to sign into your account, if you weren't already signed in, and the item begins downloading. You are given the chance to enter any promotional code you have, such as a gift certificate, before the purchase is final.

New songs and videos are added to the Purchased playlist in the iPod app (see Lesson 16) on your iPad 2.

You don't need an iTunes Store account to download audio or video podcasts or iTunes U classes. You can listen to or watch the podcast without downloading it, or download it to the iPad 2 and sync it to your iTunes library on your personal computer.

To listen, just press the podcast title. To download, press the Free button and then press Get Episode. New podcasts are added to the Podcast list in iPod (see Lesson 16), where you can listen to them or watch them. To get additional episodes in a series, press the Get New Episodes button in the Podcasts list. Video podcasts are also available in the Video app (see Lesson 15, "Playing Videos and YouTube").

> NOTE: **Using AirPlay**
>
> If you purchase the AppleTV unit, you can use AirPlay to send all sorts of content from your iPad 2 to the Apple TV device, and then onto your television. See the Apple TV documentation for details.

Using iTunes Home Sharing

iTunes Home Sharing is the kind of feature that you might never have imagined on your own—but that you might have trouble living without once you use it. With iTunes Home Sharing, you can stream content seamlessly from your Macintosh or Windows PC to your iPad (the original or the iPad 2). Your computer acts like a big library of content that your iPad can tap into at any time.

Why would you do this? Simple—when you want to use content that's on a nearby computer (on the same Wi-Fi network), you don't have to hassle with syncing content onto your iPad, or worry about using up storage on the iPad either. Your iPad becomes a viewer for your iTunes content library, one which you can use anywhere that's comfortable for you within the Wi-Fi network's range.

If you use iTunes Home Sharing, the way you use your iPad can become different. You only put content on it that you want to use when you're away from your personal computer. The rest of the time, you can just depend on your existing stored files.

Of course, it's up to you. The need to have your computer on while you view the content that's stored on it could be a turn-off (no pun intended). You can ignore iTunes Home Sharing, and leave your personal computer off while you play back files that are stored directly on your iPad. Especially if you have a large media library, though, iTunes Home Sharing is worth serious consideration.

To use iTunes Home Sharing, you need to be on a Wi-Fi network. You first bring content into iTunes on your personal computer. The process is very similar to bringing content into iTunes on your iPad 2. Or, you can sync content onto your personal computer after you have downloaded it to your iPad 2.

You then need to activate Home Sharing as a feature within Preferences for iPod. Sign in with the same Apple ID and password that you use to access iTunes. After you do so, the content on your personal computer is available via your iPad.

For instance, in the Videos app, Playback takes a few seconds to start, but is then very similar to playback from a video stored on the iPad itself.

In iTunes on your iPad, you'll find a Shared list on the left-hand side of the window. The Shared list includes music, movies, TV shows, and more. Just choose content from the Shared list to play it on your iPad.

You can also use Home Sharing to share files among the iTunes libraries of multiple computers on the same network. If you're in a location where the iTunes account is different, log in to that iTunes account instead.

NOTE: **Leaving Your Computer On**

One problem with iTunes Home Sharing is that it only works if your personal computer is on. If it's on, of course, it uses power, and it may also make noise. To avoid this kind of problem, many people are buying home servers, which can be tucked away out of sight, and out of hearing. Such devices can also be set up to run without having the monitor on, reducing power consumption.

NOTE: **Using TV and Movie Apps**

In addition to iTunes, the apps Hulu and Netflix are very popular options for bringing TV shows and movies onto your iPad 2. Both services use streaming video and work best with a Wi-Fi connection, although it's worth experimenting with 3G if you have a 3G iPad as well. (Your mileage may vary depending on your carrier, location, and so on.) For all these services, content providers have taken heed of the large and fast-growing iPad market and optimized their content for the 1024×768 screen resolution found on both the iPad and iPad 2. The result is that shows look great and stream quickly. I find skips to be rare even when using a slow Wi-Fi connection.

Getting ePub Books into iTunes

Getting ePub books into iTunes is perhaps easier to do than it is to explain. It's hard to explain because there are many sources for ePub books; it's easy to do because each step seems quite natural.

You can get an ePub book file as an email attachment or as a file that you download from a website. Simply save the file in a convenient place, such as your computer desktop.

Open iTunes and select the Books link in the Library area:

1. Obtain an ePub book file by downloading an email attachment or file that you obtain from a website to your computer.

2. Open iTunes.

3. To drag and drop the book file into iTunes, open the Books link in the Library area, as shown in Figure 18.3. Drag the ePub file into the Books area.

4. To get the file into iTunes using a dialog, choose File, Add to Library. In the Add to Library dialog box, also shown in Figure 18.3, choose the file you want to upload.

   The file is uploaded to the Books area.

FIGURE 18.3   You can select a file, or drag and drop it into iTunes.

5. Sync iTunes to your iPad 2, as described in the next section.

The book is transferred to your iPad 2.

Syncing Content with a Personal Computer

When you connect your iPad 2 to your personal computer, iTunes automatically syncs content from iPad 2 to iTunes and vice versa.

When you sync, you are not only transferring new or existing content, you are also able to manage storage on your iPad 2. Here are the types of content that you can sync with iTunes:

▶ **Media and apps**—Music, movies, TV shows, games and applications from the App Store; music videos, podcasts, and iTunes U collections; audiobooks, books, videos from your computer's movie folder or application; and photos from your computer's photo folder or application.

▶ **Personal information management**—Contacts, calendars, notes, email account settings (from personal computer to iPad 2 only), and web page bookmarks.

Follow these steps to first set options in iTunes on your personal computer, and then synchronize your iPad 2 to it:

1. Connect iPad 2 to your computer.

2. If iTunes doesn't open automatically on your personal computer, open it.

3. In iTunes, select iPad 2 in the sidebar. Tabs for managing syncing to your iPad 2 appear.

4. In the Summary tab, shown in Figure 18.4, set options for managing synchronization.

FIGURE 18.4   Use iTunes to help manage storage on your iPad 2.

Options include setting iPad 2 back to its original settings, which will erase any content on it; syncing only selected songs and videos; and manually managing songs and videos. These options are good to use if your iPad 2 is filling with content.

5. On the Info tab, set options for syncing contacts, calendars, bookmarks, and notes.

   To sync to Apple's MobileMe, click the Learn More button. Contacts, calendars, mail accounts, and/or notes can all be synced with Outlook on Windows. You can sync contacts only with Google Contacts, Windows Contacts, or Yahoo! Address Book. You can sync web browser bookmarks with Internet Explorer. You can also replace selected information on the iPad 2, on a one-time-only basis, with information from the personal computer running iTunes.

6. On the Apps tab, set options for syncing apps. You can view your apps and the storage they use, and specify which ones to keep on your iPad 2; others are stored in iTunes on your personal computer for later use if needed.

7. On the Music tab, set options for syncing music. You can sync all music or only selected playlists, artists, and genres. Unlike apps, you can't manage storage directly, but you can use these estimates to help: 1 minute of music takes up about 1 megabyte, and typical songs are about 3 minutes long, or 3MB in file size.

8. On the Movies tab, set options for syncing movies (TV shows are separate). You can automatically sync all movies or recent ones (by whether they've been watched or by number of movies), or specify which movies to sync. Specifying individual movies is probably a good idea, because each movie can take up 1GB or more of space.

9. On the TV Shows tab (see Figure 18.5), set options for syncing TV shows. As with movies, you can automatically sync all TV shows or recent ones (by whether they've been watched or by number of shows), or specify which movies to sync. Specifying individual TV shows is probably a good idea, because a one-hour show can take up half a gigabyte or more of space.

FIGURE 18.5 Managing TV show syncing helps preserve storage on your iPad 2.

10. In the Podcasts, iTunes U, and Books tabs, set options for syncing each type of media content.

Options are similar to other media described in the previous steps, with options to sync all content of a given type, recent items, or specific items. Video podcasts and books that include lots of video clips are likely to be the largest in file size.

11. On the Photos tab, set options for syncing photos and videos.

You can sync all folders or specified ones, and you can include or exclude videos. You can also place videos in folders, and then use the syncing options for those folders to manage storage requirements associated with video.

TIP: **Sync Photos Through iPad 2**

It's fun to use your iPad 2 as a photo viewer with friends and family, but keep in mind that you can't delete synced photos from the

> iPad 2 directly, which means you have to manage synced photos via iTunes on your personal computer. It may be helpful to keep a folder on your personal computer that is specified for use with your iPad 2 only.

12. From any tab where you have changed options, you can click Apply to apply the changes and start a sync. Otherwise, to start a sync using all the new settings, click the Sync button from any tab.

Summary

In this lesson, you learned about iTunes and how it works on the iPad 2 and personal computers; getting content for the iPad 2, including music and movies; and how to sync iPad 2 with a personal computer.

Now that you've completed the final lesson, you're ready to get the most out of your iPad 2. Enjoy!

Index

Q-R

Y-Z

How can we make this index more useful? Email us at indexes@samspublishing.com

FREE Online Edition

Your purchase of **Sams Teach Yourself iPad 2 in 10 Minutes** includes access to a free online edition for 45 days through the Safari Books Online subscription service. Nearly every Sams book is available online through Safari Books Online, along with more than 5,000 other technical books and videos from publishers such as Addison-Wesley Professional, Cisco Press, Exam Cram, IBM Press, O'Reilly, Prentice Hall, and Que.

SAFARI BOOKS ONLINE allows you to search for a specific answer, cut and paste code, download chapters, and stay current with emerging technologies.

Activate your FREE Online Edition at www.informit.com/safarifree

> **STEP 1:** Enter the coupon code: TXCCUWA.

> **STEP 2:** New Safari users, complete the brief registration form. Safari subscribers, just log in.

If you have difficulty registering on Safari or accessing the online edition, please e-mail customer-service@safaribooksonline.com